LIBERTIES OF THE MIND

LIBERTIES OF THE MIND

By

CHARLES MORGAN

NEW YORK

THE MACMILLAN COMPANY

1951

72817

ACKNOWLEDGEMENTS

The introductory essay on "Mind Control" has not appeared before. The Zaharoff Lecture on "The Liberty of Thought" was first published by the Clarendon Press for the University of Oxford; the W. P. Ker Memorial Lecture on "The Artist in the Community" by Jackson, Son & Co. for the University of Glasgow; and "The Liberty of Self-Renewal" and the essays here called "Instances" by *The Times Literary Supplement*. I express my grateful acknowledgements.

C. M.

CONTENTS

CHAP.   PAGE

I. INTRODUCTION: MIND CONTROL . . . 1

II. PRINCIPLES 55

    THE LIBERTY OF THOUGHT 57

    THE ARTIST IN THE COMMUNITY 81

III. INSTANCES 105

    THE DARK AGES or *The Liberty Not to Despair* . . 107

    IMAGINING THE FUTURE or *The Liberty to Build* . . 116

    MASTER AND PUPIL or *The Liberty of Teaching* . . 123

    OLD KASPAR'S WORK UNDONE or *The Liberty to Have Roots* 132

    THE GLOW OF LIVING or *Liberty in Time* . . . 141

    THE WINE AND THE BOTTLE or *The Liberty to Enjoy and Accept* 150

IV. THE LIBERTY OF SELF-RENEWAL . . . 159

    FOREWORD 161

    THE ROMANTIC IDEA 163

    ROMANTICISM IN ART 171

    ROMANTICISM AND SOCIETY 179

    MARITAIN'S CLASSICAL METHOD 187

    MARITAIN ON EQUALITY 195

    CONCLUSION 203

V. INSTANCES 207

    BERGSON AND THE MARITAINS or *Liberty from Materialism* 209

    HUMANE COUNSELLORS or *The Liberty to Ask Questions* . 217

    THE SILKWORM AND THE LOOM or *The Liberty to Mind One's Own Business* 225

    A WRITER AMONG PAINTERS or *The Liberty to Communicate* 233

    SANCTITY AND SONG or *The Liberty to Draw Back Curtains* 244

I. INTRODUCTION: MIND CONTROL

INTRODUCTION: MIND CONTROL

THE essays which follow were not written in any expectation that they would find themselves between the covers of a volume with the present title. Their unity, in my own mind at any rate, is the closer for that reason. They seem to have selected themselves and to have indicated my book's subject by their convergence upon it.

An unexpected visit to my house by an American physicist, of whom I shall speak later, was the occasion of their being gathered together. His conversation forced me to understand that power over the mind was being developed farther, and was assuming a more concrete form, than I had supposed. The effect of his words was that of a flare springing up from an aerodrome about which one has long been circling in the dusk, knowing it to be there but not clearly distinguishing it. The centre of convergence of my essays became suddenly plain. Though they were written before I had any hint of my friend's scientific project, they appeared now to have been looking towards it from their separate points of view. It has seemed right not to allow what he said to affect my revision, but to leave my essays as early witnesses to a truth that has outrun me and is, perhaps, outrunning the world.

The first in order though not in date, a Zaharoff Lecture at Oxford, treats the main problem, in the context of Montesquieu's *Esprit des Lois*, as an aspect of political philosophy; the second sees it from an artist's point of view; and at the centre of the volume will be found a group of essays, called " The Liberty of Self-Renewal ", which, in discussing the ancient conflict (and brotherhood) between Classicism and Romanticism, attempts to advance a little way towards the

3

heart of the matter.   Of the other essays, called " Instances ",
I will say only that their coming together has shown me how
often and in how many and various connexions my thought
has led me towards an acknowledgement that, in the modern
world, not only the liberties of conduct but the liberties of
the mind itself are in peril.

This is a hard and unfamiliar saying.   The reader, as I did,
will perhaps resist as long as he can the possibility of its being
true, just as " many scientists could and did hope that some
principle would emerge which would prove that atomic
bombs were inherently impossible ".*

He may say incredulously: " No one can stop me from
thinking what I like or make me think against my will."   This
pleasant belief is becoming less and less true, and the threat
of its becoming altogether untrue, the threat that the human
mind may become subject to immediate external control and
be switched on or off and turned hither and thither like an
electric torch, is the threat of an evil which is exceedingly far-
reaching.   There are many who, believing in their infallible
wisdom, would regard a power to switch the human mind as
an opportunity, not as a threat.   There are others who, while
recognizing the danger of this power's being misapplied,
would not call it evil because they will call nothing evil.   I
submit that they are mistaken and that the hour is late.

The Possibility of Control   It has, of course, never been completely and strictly true
that thought is exempt from control.   Educationists, priests
and parents have always had a limited and uncertain power to
make the child the father of the man and so, it may be said,
to create the conditions within which the man thinks.   His
later environment, the books he reads, the music he hears, the
company he keeps, all influence his thought, but these in-

* H. D. SMYTH: *Atomic Energy*.   U.S.A.   Government Printing
Office and H.M. Stationery Office, London.   (The official account,
p. 134.)

fluences, as educationists, priests and parents know to their
cost, are by no means secure; within them the human mind
has stubbornly preserved a glorious genius for going off any
rails laid down for it.   Influences such as these have been
influences at a remove.   They have never been able, though
they have tried, to possess themselves of the core of the mind
itself so that their will has become its will, their good its good,
and their evil its evil.   For this reason, these indirect influences, however powerful in particular instances, are different
in kind from the form of mind-control, arbitrary and direct
like the control of a lamp, which the world must now contemplate.

Between the educative influences and that direct and imperative mind-control which, to be clear, I shall for the time-
being speak of as Switch Control, there lie certain intermediate
controls—those exercised, for example, by hypnotists in their
kind, or by psychiatrists or anæsthetists in theirs.   I mention
them here not to associate them with Switch Control but to
distinguish them from it.

It is always taught that there is a firm limit to hypnotic
influence and that though a hypnotist can make us do, think
or remember certain things, he cannot go past the inner
defences of our beliefs or our convictions of right and wrong.
In brief, he cannot maim or transmute the personality itself,
whereas the power to transmute is essential to Switch Control.

There are rumours that hyoscyamus or some drug in that
series is used in the preparation of victims who are to give
evidence against themselves; but the authorities to whom I
have referred assure me that anæsthetics, in the ordinary meaning of the word, are completely dissociate from the idea of
Switch Control, for they produce " an oblivion, a sleep that
may be very deep, but no change in the personality as far as we
know."   This is confirmed by our common experience.   We
return from an anæsthetic with no sense of having, under its

influence, ceased to be ourselves or of there having been a fragmentation and reassembly of our personality. We have travelled elsewhere but have remained whole. We have not been maimed. Switch Control, as I envisage it, implies maiming.

I say " as I envisage it " because, in speaking of Switch Control, I make no claim to be describing a known and established method of coercing the human mind. My American visitor did not claim that a method had been established, though he did not know how far research might have gone in countries other than his own. My purpose is to open up a new field of speculation; to suggest that humanity is threatened by a new force; and to feel my way towards a preliminary understanding of it. Evidently if experiments are being made in Switch Control, their secret will be the more elaborately guarded as they become more nearly operational. Meanwhile it would be rash to claim more than that they are in the scientific air, and that we do well to observe which way the wind is blowing. My limited attempt now is to bring within the range of the reader's and of my own thought a new concept: the concept of a power to dispossess men of their minds, their wills and even their individualities, so that, by the application to John of a scientific process or " switch ", John may not only be persuaded to agree with Joe or to obey him, but may be so changed that he is no longer psychologically John but is only the bodily husk of John into which an alien psychology has been injected at Joe's discretion. The power to make this injection, like the power of nuclear energy in the early Nineteen Forties, may not as yet have advanced beyond the early or " laboratory " stages of its development. It may even remain there. Some principle may emerge to prove that direct Switch Control of the mind by electrical or other physical means is— what scientists hoped that atomic bombs might prove to be— inherently impossible. Meanwhile, to envisage the possibility, and try to understand it, is not to be an alarmist but to be awake.

Psychiatry may seem to have a closer bearing on Switch Control than either hypnotism or anæsthetics, but here again a clear distinction has to be made. According to the school of thought to which a psychiatrist belongs, psychiatry employs differing techniques, but they all rest upon a conviction, and indeed upon proof, that it is possible, in certain cases, by lightening or increasing the emphasis which the conscious mind lays upon parts of the whole mind, to correct an unbalance or distortion of the whole mind. The object is the object of all medicine: to re-enable the patient's natural health, to restore him to himself. This marks an important distinction. Psychiatry, in operating upon a mind, conceives of it as preserving its identity. The patient may be led into forgetting some things and remembering others, into cutting away with the knife of understanding the ropes which bound him to excessive fears or destructive anxieties; in this sense he is changed, but it is of his delusions, not of himself, that he is deprived. This at least is the theory. The practice may be dangerous because the nature of identity, of who John is, may be misconceived by the practitioner, but this is a metaphysical criticism which for the moment is beside the point. Psychiatry looks to and respects identity and the powers of willing and choosing, the primary liberties of the mind, which arise from it.

Switch Control, as I envisage it, will not respect these things. Its aim will be, for the subject's good or the subject's evil, for the operator's good or the operator's evil, to annihilate in a man his natural identity and to substitute for it another identity, which shall not have the faculty of individually willing or choosing. The body will have the same eyes but a different man will look out of them. Perhaps if Switch Control reaches perfection, though the eyes will move as they did before and physically see their way to the battlefield or the labour-camp, no one will look out of them.   They may be the windows of a seemingly unoccupied room.*

* Having acquired from my naval training a horror of writers who go down to the sea *on* ships and voyage therein at several knots *an hour*, and having therefore respect for other men's skills, I have submitted my sentences about psychiatry to a practising master of the subject.   He has been generous enough to add the following comment, which carries yet farther the distinction I have tried to make: " I have never thought of a psychiatrist as working out a conception of the patient's identity. He does not try to see the picture of the real man so that he can re-fashion him.   He tries to find out and, more important, to enable the sick man to find out in what way he is sick and how it came about.   This is, as you say, the ' knife of understanding ' which ' cuts the ropes ', but it is the patient's own knife and he cuts his own ropes, and, if successful and sufficiently strong, he becomes free.   It is only in this way that his identity and unity are regained.   This is the teaching of what the psychiatrist should do.   There are bound to be bad psychiatrists who use a bad technique and conceited ones who try to instil their own ideas. I suppose we all do this in some degree, being human and ready to see ourselves as gods, but the result is either to make the patient happier by a lucky chance or to make him more ill.   I can't believe that we can alter his identity, distort his fundamental personality, or maim him in the way you ascribe to Switch Control."

This strengthens my own view that Switch Control, if it exists or is about to exist, is something altogether new.   My correspondent continues:

" But, if we go on from all this, there are facts to be considered and understood and, if possible, explained.   The Russian trials show that something can be done with individuals.   Mindtzenty knew in advance that it would be done to him; the man who escaped in Bulgaria told something of the method; the medieval witch-trials showed the same sort of thing.   I don't think we know, certainly I don't know, what is the technique.   There seems to be a preparation, a breaking down and emptying of the mind such as you describe.   Fear could do it, physical or mental exhaustion could do it, there may be drugs which can do it, I don't know.   I should think that the process could be applied only to individuals and not to groups.   Isolation and the feeling of being helpless and alone are probably factors in the business."

So much for the purging and emptying of the mind.   My own theory is that means have been or are being found not only to purge the mind but to put something into it, to " possess " it.   My correspondent offers no direct explanation of this, but continues:

" *But the other fact, to my mind a more alarming one, is that we are all being conditioned to accept a limitation of freedom, even of some of our mental freedom.   Some are aware of it and try, consciously, to resist.   But I fear that, unconsciously, even we are ready to accept this new infection which could*

In order that unfamiliar argument might proceed by stages, *The Nature of Possessive Control* I have hitherto likened this power over the mind to the power of a man, holding an electric torch, to turn it on or off and direct its beam hither and thither.   The simile has become inadequate and I take leave to abandon it.   The power being sought for is not simply a power to dominate, as a torch is dominated, from the outside—for that is the familiar tale of intimidation and torture—but a power to drive a man out of his individuality, to introduce an alien tenant into the house which is his body, and, in the gospels' meaning of " possess ", to possess him.   It will be more accurate to speak of Possessive Control than of Switch Control.

What evidence is there that Possessive Control exists or, if it does not exist already, is in the process of development? There can be two kinds of evidence in this matter: factual evidence of experiment and progress; and presumptive evidence that a probability of such a development is inherent in the conditions of the modern world: in brief, that the world is sickening for this particular disease.

I bring forward what evidence I have without claiming that it proves the existence of a mechanism of Possessive Control in operation or even that an effective mechanism lies in the near future.   Nuclear physics may develop more rapidly in other directions, for there seems to be " little doubt ", as the Scientific Correspondent of *The Times* has said, " that within a few decades, if not a few years, it will be possible for any Power with modern industrial resources to destroy the world as we know it ".   In that case, there will be no more minds

---

not have harmed us before 1939.   There is no such immunity in the great mass of our people and no consciousness of danger.   They lap up the virus as though it were milk.   One can think of many ways in which the population as a whole is being conditioned or prepared for this mental change, this loss of individuality and identity."

I have italicized this passage because it is a re-statement by a man of science of the theme of this book.

to control. Meanwhile I submit that whether there exists or does not exist a physical mechanism of Possessive Control, there is overwhelming evidence that the problem of the Liberties of the Mind has moved out of the hinterland of political philosophy and is today as urgent and practical as the problem of the emancipation of slaves was in the past.

The factual evidence is scant but not negligible. It arises from the Soviet trials and, for me, from the account given by my American visitor of his own and his colleagues' scientific activity.

The Soviet Trials

It is at least certain, even from the little knowledge we have of the Soviet trials, that an effect is being produced upon the minds of prisoners different in kind from anything previously known. We have been told again and again by reliable observers that the prisoners have not the appearance of men who have been lately subjected to torture. To this some may answer: " They have been tortured, but long enough ago, or in so subtle a way that they bear no visible marks of it, and they speak as they do in horror of a renewal of torture." This answer, which might be sufficient in one or two or three instances, is not sufficient in the many instances we know of. Even if a way of torture has been found which leaves no mark or sign; even if we assume that the prisoners have been submitted to torture and are in fear of its repetition, their behaviour and the regularity of it are still explained only in part.

In court they are not actually suffering physical torture. Unless their minds are *then* being controlled, they are free to speak their own truth until a hand is clapped over their mouth and they are swept away to the torture chamber. It is not credible that none would have done so. Some of them, it is true, have been no more than gangsters repudiated by their gang. Bred in materialism, not as men having spirits, and insulated by the Soviets from the history of ideas, they have been unaware of the existence of truths worth dying for. But many of the prisoners, conspicuously the Cardinal, have not been in this ant-like category.   They have known, if they have retained the faculty of knowing, that nothing could save their bodies and that on this earth they had no more to win or lose. The Cardinal knew, if he retained the faculty of knowing, that to have spoken but one sentence of witness to his truth: Into Thy hands I commend my spirit, would have lighted such a candle as none can put out.   Yet he, like others, was compliant, and compliant in the same way with them.   It is against our knowledge of human nature, and of the long, unbroken history of martyrdom, to suppose that among so many men not one would have been found to speak his soul out.   A collapse of fortitude is not explanation enough.   Neither suffering how-ever extreme nor fear however dreadful can have produced the smooth, grey monotony of these self-accusations.   Something happens to these prisoners which, though almost certainly accompanied or preceded by torture, is not itself an exquisite development of torture as it has been formerly understood, but different in kind.   It appears to be psychological, not physiological, in principle—a process, that is to say, which does not aim at the mind through the body, but directly at a seizure, an occupation, a possession of the mind.   It appears also to have effects more precise, immediate and mechanical than are to be expected from any perversion of psychiatry.

There are other pointers to this conclusion.   The self-accusations, though they sometimes include a formal plea for mercy, are never, according to the accounts we have, an emotional outpouring, equivalent to a cry or scream.   They are quietly and calmly delivered.   Though their details vary, they appear from the reports to be uniform in style—or, rather, in their lack of it.   Each man speaks in his own voice out of his own mouth; there is no suggestion of a trance-like state; and yet he does not speak in character.

At first it seems not unreasonable to explain this by saying that the prisoners have been compelled under torture to learn a dictated part, and now, in fear of torture, are reciting it.   No doubt there is truth in that, but again the explanation is inadequate.   Men forget parts; if they are in terror, or if (in any previously known meaning of the phrase) their nervous systems have been broken down, their responses are erratic; if a hypnotic influence were being used, there would, I understand, be a risk of loosening, of interruption, of slur—even of silent sleep.   None of these explanations will serve.   When these prisoners are brought into court, their captors have absolute assurance of the result.   The prisoners are gramophones into which a record has been inserted, and yet are more responsive than gramophones, for they answer questions. For a moment Kostov appeared to come out of the groove. This may have been a consequence of mechanical error or of a deliberate attempt to blind watchful eyes to the nature, and the terrible efficiency, of the mechanism.

The word mechanism, taken alone, is probably too concrete. The system of Possessive Control is unlikely to be as yet operational without the support of torture, and, as long as that limitation remains, a part of the world may hope for a little while to be exempt from it.   But the evidence of the Soviet trials makes it hard not to believe that a method of Possessive Control is passing beyond its laboratory stages.

American Research

The possibility of this had long been in the shadow and background of my thought when my American visitor brought it into the open.   In giving an account of his visit, I shall inevitably use terms which men of science would prefer not to use, but I think it is better to employ my own non-technical language for what it may be worth than to fumble with a specialized vocabulary.

My friend is a young nuclear physicist.   As I had had no news of him for some time, I asked what he had been doing and what had brought him to Europe.   He spoke first of the ways in which atomic science may be used defensively against the pilotless carriers of atomic bombs. I will say nothing of this. He added, in reply to another question: " Well, we are giving attention more and more to the psychological field."

What did that mean? " Just that we are engaged in research on how to help the human mind. People get it all wrong when they think of physics in terms of bombs. There's that aspect but there's much more. For example, there's synthetic food, specially milk."

The word he used was not " synthetic ", but an unfamiliar word which I cannot recall and for which " synthetic " is the best substitute I can find. A discourse followed—extremely serious but with a grin in it—on the inconvenience, the wastefulness and the general redundancy of cows. " Cows ", he said, " take up too much room." It was becoming reasonable, he added, to look forward to a world without cows. . . . And without stock-raising and agriculture? I asked. . . . And without the grape? . . . Sans work, sans cows, sans wine, sans everything, and yet with all their beneficent effects.

We returned to the mind. Great progress had already been made in " the psychological field ". With what object? Well, in the first place, it might become possible to cut short the educational process. Instead of putting a child down to learn things for years and years, you'd recondition selected areas (" areas " was not the word) of his brain, so's he'd learn quicker what he wanted to learn.

Or what others wanted him to learn? I asked.

My visitor agreed briefly without taking my point. A French scientist, he said, was reported to have made an extremely interesting experiment with a frog's egg. The experiment was not as yet " documented ", and one of his own reasons for being in Europe was to investigate and, if he could, repeat and vary it. A frog's egg had outside it five areas or fields of energy which were electrically distinguishable and measurable.

(I am aware that I am now using a layman's language.)   These fields had been found to correspond with the head and the four legs of the ultimately resulting frog.   The Frenchman had discovered a means of neutralizing (this is the word my friend used but he was probably making things easy for me)—of neutralizing one of these fields.   The egg was hatched.   The tadpole appeared to be normal, but the resulting frog had but three legs.

If, my visitor argued, you could neutralize a leg before hatching, why not afterwards?   If a leg, why not the head?   If the head, why not a brain?   If the brain, why not a part of the brain?

And if, I asked, it is possible by electrical process to neutralize a selected part of the brain, to empty it of what it would otherwise have contained and to sweep and garnish it, should it not also be possible to enter into it and, so to speak, recondition it?

Why, yes, that was the whole point.   It was a long way off. To put the mind " out " was one thing.   Drugs and electric shock could do that.   To put " out " a selected part of the mind would be a great advance, but might well be within reach.   To put a mind " in " was an altogether different story and might be far away.   But yes—that was the point ultimately.   It was what he'd been thinking of when he spoke of education.   A great deal might be done, for example, to correct mental deficiency, to counteract faults of heredity, or to " effect a worth-while substitution for criminal trends ".

" What it all boils down to," he added, " is a long hope of turning bad citizens into good."

Interpreting my silence as doubt of the power of nuclear physics, he looked out across the room and said : " Ultimately, of course.   I don't suppose I shall live to see it."

I said I feared that he might.

" Fear? " he exclaimed.   " Why do you *fear* it? "

"Because," I answered, "I don't want to put it into anyone's power to turn a child into a hyena."

"Oh," he said, with a smile, "they're mostly that already," but added: "Of course I agree: any progress is open to abuse. But you can't bar progress for that reason. If you do, you don't get any place."

It was a point of view, but there were, I suggested, reasons for supposing that, in this particular instance, it was untenable. Man could risk the abuse of any other power over him but not of a power which might deprive him of the liberties of his mind; for, as long as he retained these liberties, all abuses of power were at least in theory corrigible by his exercise of them, but, when once they were gone, abuse was incorrigible and eternal. In the conditioned mind, there would be no knowledge of servitude. Passive and without self-consciousness, it would just wear out, unless by accident it jumped the groove and went screaming across the record. In that case, the controllers of the apparatus would throw it away.

That, my friend conceded, was also a point of view. "And what do you suppose," he asked, "would happen then? In the end one controlled herd would over-run the other controlled herds, and there would be a single control. What then?"

I replied at a hazard that the controllers of the human apparatus might die of boredom, science having no more records to put on.

We discussed the prospect until his quest of the three-legged frog could be no longer delayed. At the door he turned back. His countrymen have the gift of admitting ideas rapidly. It is their danger and their strength; it makes them vulnerable and sometimes too volatile, but it enables them to grasp and use unfamiliar notions with astonishing speed. They can be shocked by a new idea, as we all may be if, opening our front door to go out in the ordinary course of our business, we find a stranger standing there, but the American impulse is not to slam the door of prejudice against him, but to invite him in and tame him and learn from him and put him to use.   My friend must have been shocked at first by my criticism of his eagerness; but now, his hand on the latch, he looked at me through his glasses and said, with that penetrating and generous directness which is a distinguishing quality of first-rate American minds and has in it the saving naïveté of Tolstoy's Pierre: " It all depends, doesn't it, not so much on what one thinks that men can do as on what one believes that a man is ? "

It was a pregnant saying from an agnostic in full revolt against a puritanical upbringing.   For a moment I hoped that, as Pierre might have done, he would forget his frogs and come back to the fire with me.   But he did not; there was a train to catch.   That is one of the outstanding differences between Americans and Russians : Americans catch trains, and, unlike the characters of Tchekov, when they try to commit suicide they frequently succeed.

The Mind's Tendency to Surrender

Whether or not he and his colleagues are able to perfect a machine with power over the mind, whether or not a machine of this nature already exists, the idea of it may serve as a focus of thought.   It stands like a door at the end of a narrowing passage down which mankind is now visibly walking, with a surrender at each step of more and more of the liberties of the mind.   This is what was meant by saying that the world was " sickening for this particular disease ".

Surrender has been in part unconscious, in part willing and even enthusiastic.   The process may be traced back as far as the middle of the eighteenth century, but has been accelerated in the nineteenth and twentieth.   A scientific historian who examined its development would perform valuable service, but he would need courage and detachment, for the liberty of the mind is a subject that cuts across every party and sectarian alignment among non-totalitarian peoples.   It is, indeed, among the deepest issues of our time, but only now is it becoming clearly distinguishable through the disguises with which sometimes selfishness and sometimes progressive good-will have shrouded it.

Two great forces, each in itself potentially beneficent, have, during the nineteenth century and our own, chiefly contributed to a gradual and scarcely perceived surrender of this essential liberty: man's increasing sense of communal responsibility, and his newly developed powers over Nature. Each produced a revolution in thought of extreme violence. Man's social conscience and his notion of his place in the universe were both transformed. He was like the captain of a ship who, struck in harbour by ferocious storms, finds that his moorings are dragging, casts them off, and puts out, because he must, into an uncharted sea.

So high was his spirit that he saw the voyage as one of adventure and discovery. A passionate expectation—which we now too easily disparage as optimism—for a time sustained him; at least it kept him on the bridge. The tempests which had so fiercely driven him beyond the areas of his previous experience, as Greek mariners long ago were driven off their familiar shores, combined to produce that concept of progress by which the noblest and most active minds of the nineteenth century were animated. But many of these minds were also tormented by it, and by their ever-increasing sense that not only were they losing their former power to steer their ship but that they had lost their bearings and were cut off from their spiritual origins. " The night is dark and I am far from home."

Any attempt to distinguish the attitude of men of the nineteenth century towards their special predicament must lead to generalization of a kind which, accurate historians tell us, ought not to be hazarded. Who were " the men of the nineteenth century "? Had they a distinguishable " attitude "?

In using such terms are we not confusing the issue? And yet to say that our grandfathers' and our fathers' attitude was different from our own is not to talk nonsense; the proposition is felt to be true; and if a difference between two generalizations is felt to be historically real, it cannot be historically illegitimate to attempt those generalizations.

The Nineteenth-century Dilemma

To Englishmen of, let us say, Tennyson's generation, whose childhood emerged from the Regency and whose coming-of-age was marked by the Reform Bill of 1832, the storm appeared at first as being rather political than scientific. To those of my own father's kind, who appeared in the world when Queen Victoria had already been on the throne some twenty years, the emphasis was reversed, for by the time they were young men Chartism, the Hungry Forties and Catholic Emancipation were far behind, freedom had really begun to look as if it might broaden down from precedent to precedent, and it was widely believed that increased speed of communications was an almost unmixed blessing which would lead to peace between nations. There was a brief period, as the Eighties turned into the Nineties, to which, if we are thinking chiefly of the professional, the administrative and the lower middle classes, the word complacent is not inapplicable in England, in America, and even in France, where the Third Republic was settling down more comfortably than had seemed likely.

Economically and scientifically it was an expanding age. Competition was fierce, but there had never been so widespread an opportunity for talent and hard work or so firm an assurance that reward, once earned, could be maintained and multiplied. Thrift and enterprise were twin virtues, for it was not the policy of any state to drive men to the instant spending of what they earned by the fear that all they saved would be taken from them or that the currency would violently depreciate. It was considered as legitimate to defer one's spending for a year or ten years or a lifetime as to defer it for a week.

To provide by immediate self-sacrifice for one's own old age or for one's own wife and children was not considered an anti-social act. It was felt, and rightly felt, that, though extremes of poverty remained, gigantic advances had been made and were continuing to be made in the direction of social justice. A confident looking-forward had become, among millions of men, a habit of mind. This may be called complacency, but we may hesitate to call it so unless we are sure that our own folly is not a cause of its having been unjustified by the event.

It may be said that these " complacent " ones ought to have foreseen what would become of their accumulation and their hopes, and should have been aware that there was in their ointment a fly that would breed. Many of them were uneasily and some fully aware of it. In the history of nineteenth-century thought a struggle between confidence and unease is never absent for long. That the idea of progress, as it presented itself in its political and scientific aspects, was capable of being turned to good effect few dared permit their conscious minds to doubt. To recognize, as we do now, that the new chapter in the human experiment might well be the last was not often possible to men of the period. Those who did recognize this probability were often visited by the agonies of gloom which appear continually amid the heartiness, the pious back-slapping and the hedonistic pipe-smoking of nineteenth-century biography. It was a gloom different from our modern despairs in that it was as far as possible repressed and concealed, never cultivated as a means of self-pity and self-justification. Those who battled against it and lost, sometimes paid their penalty in madness or suicide or premature death. But they fought valiantly while they could. The idea of continuity prevailed.

> Say not the struggle nought availeth,
> The labour and the wounds are vain,

wrote Clough in the most living monument to his brave, defeated life, and his contemporaries clung passionately to a belief that all would somehow be well or might by their effort or by their prayer be made well.

Nevertheless, the struggle between confidence and unease was unremitting.   For a time it was complicated by the opposition, or supposed opposition, between evolutionary theory and the ecclesiastical orthodoxies.   This, where it was seen as a war to the death between science and religion, distracted good men and acute intellects from the real issue.   But Tennyson was little distracted by it, and Tennyson, in his strength and weakness, above all in the nature of his self-division, was as representative of his age as genius—which, in a sense, because it is genius, is essentially unrepresentative—can ever be.   " To those who used Darwin's theory," his grandson tells us,* " in support of the materialist argument, he would reply: ' I think we are something more than our skeletons. If so, it doesn't matter what those skeletons are derived from ' " —a remark which, though equally unsatisfying to both extremists in the Darwinian dispute, was at least a firm dismissal of an irrelevance.   The problem of the nineteenth century and of the years ahead struck much deeper, and Tennyson knew it, for the problem was active within him.

In his more hopeful moods, he expressed a widespread tendency of the public mind which we may call brave or complacent as we choose.   The relatively static conditions of early eighteenth-century society would not return.   The whole past, wherein man's speed of movement had been limited to that of a horse and his muscles had been aided by only very simple machines and a primitive use of explosives, was gone for ever.   The ship of his destiny had indeed dragged its moorings and struck out into unknown and stormy seas.   Somehow the storm must be, and—so confi-

* CHARLES TENNYSON: *Alfred Tennyson*, p. 486.

dence shouted or hope whispered—would be ridden out.   A
sense of communal responsibility would lead to " a Parliament
of Man, a Federation of the World ", and, as human wisdom
steadily increased its power over Nature, the great world
would spin, with ever-accumulating speed and cheerfulness,
" down the ringing grooves of change ".   Science could be
relied upon to provide the wealth which social reform would
justly redistribute.   Though it was true that the swift and at
first unregulated advances of the Industrial Revolution had
upset the former balance of communal life, a new balance
would be created, on a higher level of prosperity, by giving
expression, through an extended franchise, to a new social
conscience, and the dangers of extending the franchise would
be met by education.

The theory was not untenable.   Given time, it might have
worked out.   Gladstone and Disraeli cannot be blamed for
having failed to take account either of the impatience to which
two wars would goad the democracies or of the sudden and
deadly incontinency of Nature.   But they knew that something was wrong.   " The next fifty years are very dark on all
sides," Gladstone said to Tennyson,* and Tennyson himself,
as time went on, saw clearly that education was by no means
keeping step with the franchise.†   He saw much more than
that.   He saw that materialism had within it the germ that
would destroy even its own purposes and was already destroying them.   In 1886, his grandson says, " he was more than
ever obsessed by the thought that the world was standing on
the brink of a revolution such as had never been seen before—
' a last dim battle of the West ' which, if it came, would be
world wide."   Then follows, in Tennyson's own words, this
visionary passage: " When I see society vicious and the poor
starving in great cities, I feel that it is a mighty wave of evil
passing over the world, but that there will be yet some new

* CHARLES TENNYSON: *Alfred Tennyson*, p. 460.   † *Ibid.* p. 477.

and strange development which I shall not live to see. . . . You must not be surprised at anything that comes to pass in the next fifty years."

This was said at a time, when the Eighties were turning into the Nineties, which has already been spoken of as perhaps deserving at least a part of the reproach borne in the word complacent; and yet no words could convey more clearly a premonition of disaster. This premonition was founded in Tennyson upon an increasingly active sense, as he looked back upon his long experience, that the two great revolutions, political and scientific, had taken a wrong turning, and that loss outweighed gain. The idea was expressed in *Sixty Years After*, in which an old man looked back upon " the failure of so many of his youthful hopes for the future of the world, the gradual passing of the old social order in which he had been brought up, and the growth of a soulless commercialism ".*
It is significant that this criticism of life was at once attacked by Liberals, not in the ordinary way of literary discussion, but as a heresy. If the attack had been made by party-hacks only, it would have been unimportant, but it was delivered with passionate and nervous sincerity by honest men. The force behind it was not simply a fear that Tennyson's huge influence, using a tone of disillusionment, might damage the party. The higher liberal criticism sprang from a genuine feeling that the poet had betrayed the *ʒeitgeist* and that to do so was morally wrong; it sprang also from that inward unease in the critic, an agonized sense that the work criticized is right, which always stirs criticism to its wilder indignations.

The poem, Sir Charles Tennyson says, " seemed to be a deliberate repudiation of all the social and economic progress of the last half-century ". Such criticism could not be permitted. The thought that progress had engendered a poison within it was hardly endurable, and was the less endurable

* CHARLES TENNYSON: *Alfred Tennyson*, p. 491.

because it laid wide open the hopefully concealed split in the nineteenth-century mind—including Tennyson's own. Gladstone himself, though his manners were too good to allow him to be anything but courteous to the heretic, came down into the arena to do battle with the heresy, arguing, with all his subtlety, that Tennyson was not to be taken as having meant what he said, for the poem was purely subjective and not an "authoritative estimate" of the reforms adopted by Parliament since 1842. Of these reforms he thought it worth while to give a catalogue.

Gladstone had adroitly missed the point. Tennyson knew all about the reforms. He had approved and still approved of most of them, but, as poet and seer, he knew that, in spite of them or perhaps as a growth within them, a seed of corruption was putting out its runners over society, or, in his own words, that "a mighty wave of evil" was passing over the world. Gladstone himself had said in private almost the same thing in almost the same words. Tennyson's wrongdoing consisted in his having said it in public, for it was fast becoming progressive doctrine that in Gadara one must not talk of evil spirits within or of steep places ahead. "Justice does not require," wrote Gladstone, "nay rather she forbids, that the Jubilee of the Queen be marred by tragic notes."

Forbids! the very word is like a knell. Hitherto it had been the old guard that had prosecuted Benjamin Jowett for heresy in the Vice-Chancellor's Court at Oxford. Now the progressives themselves were adopting an attitude of moral indignation towards any criticism of their conventional thinking. They were not content to disagree with Tennyson or, as good party-men, to persuade the people to disagree with him. What had been opinion was becoming creed. They, who believed themselves to be advocates of freedom of speech and freedom of worship and had indeed done service in these causes, were moving unconsciously into a position from which

the much subtler freedom of thought was in future to be challenged and beaten down.   They were failing to preserve
clearly in their minds a distinction necessary to civilization—
namely, the distinction between disagreeing with an opponent
and treating his opposition as heretical.

If I say to a man: "I disagree with you", my words imply
that he may be right, although, thinking him wrong, I shall
do what I can, within the law, to prevent him from translating
his opinion into action.   My claim is to limit his behaviour,
not to forbid a process of his mind.   But if I say: "You are
heretical", my words imply that he is wrong absolutely and
outcast from truth.   I have raised the issue between us from
the level of reason to the level of faith, and, apart from any
action of his, have refused to allow a possible validity to a
process of his mind.   The Gladstonians had not reached this
point in their criticism of one whose interpretation of history
and whose reading of life differed from their own; they were
far from being totalitarians and even farther from detecting the
smell of totalitarianism in their own breath; but with their
suggestion that " justice forbade " anyone to strike a tragic or
discordant note in the chorus of popular self-satisfaction, they
were preparing the way for that kind of mass-mental-con-
formity which today, even among peoples who believe themselves to be free, is so widespread that it is scarcely noticed.

The final and perhaps the most striking oddity of the attack
on Tennyson is that he was accused of pessimism, whereas, to
us, in its long-term view of the future, *Sixty Years After*
appears to be one of the most optimistic poems ever written.
Sir Charles has wisely chosen to quote these most Tennysonian
lines:

Ay, for doubtless I am old, and think gray thoughts, for I am gray:
After all the stormy changes shall we find a changeless May?
After madness, after massacre, Jacobinism and Jacquerie,
Some diviner force to guide us thro' the days I shall not see?

When the schemes and all the systems, Kingdoms and Republics fall,
Something kindlier, higher, holier—all for each and each for all?
All the full brain, half brain races, led by Justice, Love and Truth;
All the millions one at length with all the visions of my youth?
All diseases quenched by Science, no man halt, or deaf, or blind,
Stronger ever born of weaker, lustier body, larger mind?
Earth at last a warless world, a single race, a single tongue—
I have seen her far away—for is not Earth as yet so young?—
Every tiger madness muzzled, every serpent passion kill'd,
Every grim ravine a garden, every blazing desert till'd,
Robed in universal harvest up to either pole she smiles,
Universal ocean softly washing all her warless Isles.

To some this may appear to be, in certain respects, a tame
and tedious prospect. They may shrink a little from the
notion of finding everywhere the same people making the
same remarks while dispassionately cultivating the same
ravine. But what can have been the liberal objections to it?
First, presumably, that the rationalist section of the party
disliked Tennyson's theism. They considered it a slur upon
their own plans for Utopia to invoke " some diviner force to
guide us " towards it. But this consideration cannot have
swayed the Gladstonians, who had always welcomed a heavenly
collaborator. " Something kindlier, higher, holier " might
well have served them, with certain Treasury reservations, as
a motto. What appears to have troubled them was Tennyson's use of question-marks. There were six in the passage
quoted, and they implied not only that Radicalism had not yet
achieved the visions of its youth but that, without miraculous
aid, it might never do so. Tennyson was undeniably still
looking for an earthly Utopia, but his question-marks suggested a doubt of the power of Science and the Franchise to
bring it about. It was necessary to deny the existence of this
doubt, and to forbid expression of it, precisely because it was
an undercurrent in so many minds.

This confusion in Tennyson's critics would be less interest- *Tennyson's*
ing than it is, and would bear less closely on our modern *Personal*
problem of the liberties of the mind, if it had not been accom- *Struggle*

panied by a confusion in the poet himself.   His confusion was different from theirs but was rooted in the same unease.

Tennyson's poetry—whenever he was not drawn by his earnest friends into doing what they, and he at last, considered his civic duty—was in its origin idealistic, was governed that is to say by his sense of idea within appearances and by his desire to seize in poetry that essence of things with which naturalism in art does not concern itself.   This was so true that it enabled him to perceive, through every kind of social and moral prejudice and in spite of active distaste, the mystical element in Baudelaire.   As the years went on, he became more and more convinced that this world is unreal, that only the spirit is real, and that the evil which he felt as " a wave " consisted in men's increasing blindness to this truth.   To hold this belief and, at the same time, to believe that men's collective exercise of their power through political institutions or scientific development had "reality" was not logically possible; and yet the two opposed beliefs—one that the Kingdom of God is within the soul, the other that human " schemes and systems " may raise up Utopia in a purgatorial world—struggled continuously in Tennyson for reconciliation.   There were times when he saw with painful clearness, and times when he would not permit himself to see, that the commandment to love one's neighbour is neither a commandment to believe in his or one's own perfectibiiity by works nor an assurance that the idea of continuous social progress is, or can by human endeavour be made, historically valid.

Its Representative Character   This struggle—or, rather, a special development of it, for the struggle itself is age-long—was characteristic of nineteenth-century thought.   Two views of " what man is "— that he is a spiritual being and that he is a progressive political animal—fought for ascendancy, or for reconciliation.   The perfected expression on earth of the first view was the contemplative life lived either within an enclosed religious order or, in the words of Kabir, " in the midst of all thine activities ". The second view was to be expressed in a life devoted to the hastening and ordering of an earthly community which, though variously defined by different progressive schools, was consistently thought of as being a product of man's rational ingenuity. Some considered that these views were mutually exclusive; some that they could be reduced to harmony; and some, like Tennyson, hating extremes and yet finding harmony unattainable, allowed the two views to exist discordantly in their minds.

These stresses had often spectacular consequences. A belief that the two opposed views of what man is were irreconcilable led, in one direction, towards the Roman Communion, and, in another, beyond agnosticism, into a positive and aggressive atheism. The hope of reconciling the two views of man's being was a ruling impulse of the Christian Socialism of Charles Kingsley and F. D. Maurice. The third approach to the problem, that of allowing the discord to remain and of striking sometimes an optimistic and sometimes what Gladstone called a " tragic " note, was Tennyson's. In him it was not cowardly or hypocritical. If it had been, it would have produced bad verse more often than it did, and would never have produced great poetry. It was, in him, a natural approach; the result of intuitions which, though their conflict preserved tension within him, he had no tendency, intellectual or temperamental, to press to logical conclusions. Because his alternating approach to the nineteenth-century dilemma had the appearance of being also the undeliberate compromise of millions, it gave to the poet, when his poetry had cast its spell, a representative character, a kind of monumental centralism, which no other poet has ever possessed in his lifetime. The waves of controversy beat fiercely against Tennyson but could not shift him. Though continually attacked by extremists for betrayal of the *ʒeitgeist*, that is to say for being in one way or another what would now be called uncontemporary, he stood unshaken because he was rooted not in the superficiality but in the deep earth of his times.

*Independ-
ence
Appears
as Guilt*For this reason it has seemed important to dwell upon him and upon the nature of the attacks made upon his work. The attackers, it has been suggested, were driven into a position of orthodoxy and heresy-hunting from which, without knowing it, they threatened the liberties of the mind. This, it may be said, was historically no new thing; other orthodoxies had pursued other heresies in the past. But in this case there were two conditions of rare significance: that the attackers knew so little what they were doing; and that there was, even in Tennyson, and certainly in the millions who felt themselves represented by him, a new and strange tendency to submit, a feeling that it was morally right to be in the swim, an obscure sense of there being something guilty in independence and something almost mutinous in not running before the wind. Tennyson was by no means a timid conformist; on the contrary he was a " character " who had a short way with those who molested him; whenever he could he escaped from general doctrinal problems, whether of religion or of sociology, to yield himself to what really interested him—his longing to be assured of the personal survival of those he loved; but to study his life and his work is to be made aware of how easy it was for men of crusading mind, whose crusade was leftward, to distract him from his dramatic and lyrical idealism, his natural desire to tell stories and sing songs and see visions through them, and to make him feel guilty and " out of it " if he did not socialize his art.

If this sense of guilt had influence upon him, how much greater was its influence upon the millions to whom the franchise, education, an expanding economy and the visible glories of applied science were offering more and more power, and into many of whose minds there had entered religious doubts which, though extremely painful to men and women of pious upbringing, came even to them in the guise of an advanced, a fashionable, and—most important of all—an open-minded malady. This " open-mindedness " of religious doubting hid from those visited by it the close-mindedness of the reception they gave to the political and scientific revolutions. The point, at the moment, is not whether this reception was wise or unwise, but that it was uncritical. Those who disliked what was happening would often plead for mitigation of the accompanying hardships. Their social conscience was not at ease, and yet it seems to be true that a part of their critical faculty, its power of radical inquiry into the virtue of change, became dulled.

They would, for example, demand improvement of conditions in factories and say: let not the bad and the cruel accompany the good; but there were few except the machine-breakers to wonder whether the " good " of applied science did not cover the potentialities of a fiend. Such criticism as there was—William Morris's, for example—presented itself to many as mere crankiness, or, alternatively, as springing from self-interest—from squires who did not want their parks spoiled, from farmers jealous for agriculture and the old rural dispensation, from the Canutes, in brief. In 1864, the Papal Encyclical *Quanta Cura* turned an uncompromising beam upon the tendencies of the times, and in 1872 Butler's *Erewhon* made its searching comment; but neither could persuade the world to be deeply critical of what was going on. Butler might as well have shouted at fish in the sea. Men had begun to think in terms of the flowing tide of progress, a dangerous habit in little fishes who may be left high and dry.

It is not to be supposed that men and women born before Waterloo and, like Tennyson, bred to a Christian tradition

and to classical learning, were insensitive to a new manifestation
of evil or unaware of the huge disproportion between human
wisdom and human power which was growing upon the race,
but they could do nothing. The storm was upon them.
Their anchors were dragging. There was nothing they could.
do but pay out cable and, in the end, slip. And as they fell
away into death, there arose, in the second half of the century,
a generation, my father's, which, sometimes eagerly and sometimes reluctantly, based its criticism of life on new premises.
Tories or Radicals, Christians or Atheists, they took it for
granted—with the exception of a few who were generally
regarded as eccentrics—that the political revolution expressed
in an ever-extending franchise and the scientific revolution
expressed in an ever-increasing power over nature were
balancing forces, like the forces of the helm and the wind
when a ship is tacking, and inherently good in that their
resultant was a forward movement. They differed ener-
getically about the speed at which the franchise should be
extended and the degree of ruthlessness with which the
scientific revolution should be applied to the breaking down
of the old life; they were fiercely divided in defence of or
attack upon what some called religion and some superstition;
they quarrelled with one another, within accepted limits, about
the course to be steered and the speed of the ship, but very
few found it in their hearts to say, or even in their minds to
suppose, what we know to have been true—that the ship was
not answering her helm and that there was a devil in the wind.

Consequent Shrinkage of the Mind's Liberties   It is necessarily hard for any man to know when he is sur-
rendering a part of the liberties of his mind. He can recognize
constraint upon his actions or upon that expression of opinion
which is itself an action, but there is for him no self-criticism
more difficult than the recognizing that within the house of
his mind, in which he believes himself to move freely, certain
rooms are locked of which he has surrendered the keys. But

the difficulty of recognizing this in himself may be lessened if
he looks into the minds of his forefathers and says: " This
thing happened to them as a consequence of certain pressures
they endured.   May it not be happening to me, upon whom
like pressures fall with ever increasing intensity? "

It is for this reason, and not with any intention of making
the men of the nineteenth century scapegoats for us, that it
has seemed worth while to suggest that there was in our forefathers a closing, a shutting off, of that part of their minds
which would have enabled them to criticize their situation
au fond and perceive in it the dreadful continuity of nineteenth-
and twentieth-century history.   They had locked the room in
their house where this monstrous knowledge awaited them
and had written on the outside of it the word Progress. Tennyson, walking in the garden, looked sometimes into the window
of that room, and recoiled from it:

> Are God and Nature then at strife,
> That Nature lends such evil dreams?

Perhaps he saw there the three-legged frog, in whom the
genius of Nature was perverted to the maiming of Nature, or
watched the Gorgons of Science pass eternally one uniform
and conditioned brain from skull to skull.   Was Man, Nature's
" last work . . . who battled for the True, the Just ", to be
nothing after all or " seal'd within the iron hills "?

> No more?   A monster then, a dream,
> A discord.

Tennyson was looking deeply then into the shut room, but
he could not continue to look at what he saw.   Neither he
and his generation nor their successors would allow themselves
to contemplate for long this particular area of the human predicament.   They would ask: " Is the evolutionary theory in
conflict with Christian belief? "   They would ask, as separated and self-balancing questions: " How can we mitigate the

suffering which the industrial revolution has brought with it?"
or " How can we ensure that the extended franchise shall be
wisely used?" but they would not allow themselves to ask:
" Are these two revolutions not self-balancing? Are they
on the contrary working together to overset the balance of
the human personality? Is it possible that, within the indis-
putable good of Progress, there is a profound evil using the
good as its instrument? Is there a devil in the wind?"
When this thought escaped into the corridors of their mind,
they drove it back, and enclosed it in a distant room, and
locked the door.

Numerical
Thinking   Why did they, bold thinkers in so much else, surrender this
part of their liberty? New pressures fell upon them, all of
which are increased upon us. They were submitted, as no
previous generation had been in the history of the world, to
what may be called numerical pressure. The drift from
country to town brought it about that the population was
thought of, and thought of itself, less and less as individuals
gathered in groups small enough not to submerge individuality,
and more and more as units of a numerical mass. In the past,
the inhabitants of Athens or of Florence had been thought of
as having an Athenian or a Florentine reality arising from the
associations of history and place. Now such associations
were dimmed and numbers began to be thought of as having
reality in themselves, a merely aggregate and numerical reality.

The distinction is hard to make, but it is a real distinction
upon which much depends. In earlier times, the internal
relationships of society had been governed, for better and for
worse, by " village " thinking or " town " thinking, or by
thinking in terms of men's trades or degrees. The result had
been a mingling of kindness with cruelty, of justice with injustice, of personal responsibility with personal privilege, which
we are all free to admire or to condemn. Whatever the bias

of our criticism, it will be useful to notice that the social system arising from these relationships was in essence customary; the law, in great part, was customary law; and this custom, sometimes oppressive and sometimes liberating, emerging from feudal times when each man had been thought of as having rights and duties according to his degree, was in origin and still in effect human. Sometimes cruelly or greedily human, but still human—not impersonal. Numerical thinking dehumanized, and perhaps one should add despiritualized, men's relationship with their fellow-men. Expressed in terms of social conditions, the effect was at first an added harshness which produced, in time, remedial but necessarily impersonal legislation. A grey soullessness appeared in societies under numerical pressure. It caused men, at all levels, to think of others and even of themselves too easily as anonymous members of vast statistical groups, and much less easily than in the past as knowable, distinguishable beings who had, each one, been a boy or a girl, who was happy or lonely or afraid, whose hand one might touch and whose look one might recognize: men and women who were, in brief, not " employers " or " employed ", not dim categories, but creatures, each *one* a child of God.

It followed that as numerical thinking affected men's regard of their fellow-men so it affected their estimate of opinion. Opinion began, as it were, to clot, and value to be attached to the fact of its being clotted. As a bead of quicksilver is drawn into a great pool of it, so individual judgement had a tendency to identify itself with the general.

At this point another distinction must be carefully made. It is one thing to say that, in a democracy, the more numerous opinion should, in the choosing of policy, prevail over the less numerous. In accepting this proposition, a member of the minority, for practical reasons that seem good to him, consents that the majority, with whom he disagrees, shall

restrict his actions.   It is an altogether different thing to say
that the more numerous opinion is, as opinion, the better
because it is the more numerous, or indeed that opinion derives
any validity at all from the fact of its being numerous.   To
accept either of these propositions is to surrender a liberty of
thought.   There is effect but no virtue in numbers.   The
earth was not the less round because everyone said that it
was flat.

*The
Clotting
of Opinion*   The power of clotted opinion to affect private judgement,
which had always existed even in small and separated communities, was swollen by the conditions of the nineteenth
century.   As communications became easier, the clot spread.
An independent mind, which formerly would have advanced
steadily by way of leisurely thought, accumulated personal
observation and the quiet reading of books, towards an independent conclusion, was continually buffeted by intrusions of
the numerical mind, by what appeared as " public opinion " or
" solid " or " reactionary " or " advanced " or merely " fashionable " opinion.   " It is widely believed " or " it is now
generally denied " were phrases that began to accumulate
about themselves respectable halos.   Not indeed that everyone
respected them.   There were many still to say: " Don't you
take as gospel all you see in them newspapers ", and we know
that Tennyson deplored in himself a habit of reading " period-
icals ".   But his protests and simpler men's sceptical, laughing
disclaimers had in them an element of defiance, and this defiance
was itself a recognition of a new, pervasive power.   Others
made little resistance.   Their small beads of quicksilver swam
into the collective clot.

There being at that time no films, no wireless in men's
homes, and no loud-speakers in the streets or in public vehicles,
the pressure of clotted opinion upon private minds was less
than it has since become.   It was at least still necessary to read

a periodical before accepting opinion from it, and this reading called for independent mental exercise. Headlines were few and brief; their object was to call attention to the text, not to act as substitutes for it; and the text, whether news or comment, was not fragmented so that its fragments might be re-arranged as tit-bits in an order of the readers' collective appetites, but began at the beginning of a narrative or argument and went on, in order of time or order of logic, at any rate in some perceptible order, until the end. A reader was assumed to be able and willing to keep his mind on a subject for long enough to take in several lines consecutively. That is changed.

Not only was the mechanism of numerical pressure weaker *Our* than it is today but men's natural resistances to it were stronger. *Weakened Resistances* If they could read at all, they had read the Bible. If they could not read, and newspapers influenced them, as was often the case, only through readings-aloud, still they had listened to the Bible, and had a language and a stock of allusions which, if I may put it so, preserved variety in their communications, and made them scorners of catchwords. Moreover, the Bible, apart from its being a sacred book and from its power to release its readers from that poverty of thought which is inherent in poverty of language, had the quality of poetry, which is an imaginative flux; and, within limits set by its being so often thought of as contained within sacred brackets, the perspective-giving quality of history.

These Bible-readers had, during the first half of the nineteenth century, another source of resistance to numerical pressure in their freedom from a standardized system of education. Such a system, when it came, brought many advantages. With all its crudities, it was necessary in industrialized communities as a palliative. To introduce and try to improve it was inevitable. But the absence of it had been a freedom none the less, for minds treated in large groups with standard doses of instruction acquire a habit of accepting conventions of thought: the palliative drug weakens the patient's natural resistances. At high levels—high in the sense of being individualistically tutorial—education is an enablement of the liberties of the mind as long as it is not compulsory; at low levels, where it can address itself only to imparting a little knowledge without enabling free criticism of the knowledge imparted, it may become dangerous in proportion to its departure from the three relatively uncontroversial Rs. No fact that a teacher can teach has meaning or value except in association with other facts; no association of facts has meaning or value except in interpretation; and an educational system which, for administrative reasons of overcrowding in time and space, or for well-intentioned reasons of vocational utility, or for the always base reason of propaganda, enforces or " advertises " or " plugs " a particular interpretation instead of using the Socratic method of inquiry, is to that extent invalid. The men of the nineteenth century, though enforcement of this kind worked upon them increasingly as the years advanced, were less subject to it than are our own contemporaries.

Ruskin's Opposition to Numerical Thinking

It is, then, on the face of it surprising that both the common people and men of Tennyson's quality were as strongly influenced by numerical pressure as in fact they were. There appear to be two interlocking explanations: their sense of guilt, sometimes social, sometimes personal, and the split in their minds between nostalgic and progressive ways of thought.

Guilt, which has already been spoken of in the context of Tennyson, is a recurrent theme in letters and biographies of the period, particularly among evangelicals and protestants of strictly puritanical upbringing. Perhaps as a consequence of the emphasis so often laid upon the Old rather than the New Testament, the wrath of God howled like a gale in men's minds. They acknowledged his love also, but as a child may remember the sun when he lies awake in terror of the dark: it did not disperse the shadows or quiet the gale.

A hundred years ago, in the middle of the century, there was no teaching to which the progressive *élite* of England, followed by eager sections of the general public, was more responsive than Ruskin's. Later the Ruskinian movement narrowed, but the reasons for its failure to carry the great public with it are as significant as the reasons for its early promise. As long as it was possible to interpret him as a supporter of the doctrine that modernism was good in itself, opinion went with him. As soon as he called into question in *Unto This Last* the economics of fashionable liberalism, and later still when he began to feel a satanic breath in the progressive wind, he was attacked as Tennyson was to be attacked for sounding " tragic notes " in the year of Jubilee.

Ruskin's economic criticism was precisely that against which his progressive contemporaries had shut their minds. They were prepared to mitigate by philanthropy and other expedients the cruelties of the prevailing system, but they would not admit that the system was bad because it was rooted in numerical thinking or, as Ruskin put it, because it dehumanized the natural relationships of society and led men to think of one another as economic units.

There were a few who grasped Ruskin's truth. We know now that *Unto This Last* was a sacred book in the early days of socialism, before socialism itself was eaten into by the numerical blight. " When the Labour Movement ", Mr. Quennell writes,* " at length became an important force in England, inquiry among its leaders and members established the fact that *Unto This Last* had had a wider and deeper influence upon their way of thinking than any other volume." The fact is not surprising. The teaching that man is not an economic unit lay at the root of the Movement and gave it its

* PETER QUENNELL: *John Ruskin.*

moral strength. It gave also to the ideals of non-Marxian Labour, as Ruskin clearly saw, common ground with the Tory view of society as an organization of personal relationships. That the teaching has been to so great an extent submerged by the alien and enemy principle of Marx is the tragic consequence of a force which has driven out of its course not the Labour Movement alone but the whole of civilization—the same force of numerical thinking which has distracted the world and defeated its good-will.

Signific-ance of Ruskin's Defeat

The strange fate of Ruskin is in other ways an illuminant of his age and of ours. By nature an æsthete and a man of nostalgic temperament who could not without agony wrest himself away from the associations of childhood, he discovered guilt even in his own enjoyment of beauty as such, and, in compensation, built his æsthetic on ethical ideas of progress. He too was driven.

Writing of him as he was in 1852, Mr. Quennell says:

Henceforward the pangs of an exacting social conscience, which derived both from a sense of guilt and a conviction of superiority, were to war against Ruskin's peace of mind, and intensify and exaggerate his fundamental restlessness.

And earlier, in speaking of the public response to Ruskin, he points out the " many obvious claims to general popularity " of his teaching in *Modern Painters*:

In a period enamoured of its own achievements, convinced that the nineteenth century represented a critical, perhaps a concluding, stage in the history of human progress, the book . . . was bound to receive the suffrage of many progressive and patriotic readers.

This is a comment on the times, the truth of which may be developed a little farther.

The period was afraid, as well as enamoured, of its own achievements. They were symbols of its guilt as well as of its power. They marked a departure from " home " as well as an advance towards a glorious and progressive manhood.

In the men and women of the period, the sense of guilt increased the stress between their nostalgic and their progressive tendencies, and this stress, in its turn, assuming a sociological form, both intensified their sense of guilt and, in doing so, submerged ideas of being in ideas of conduct.   The mysterious forces of their age converged upon and drove them.   The material needs and the swarming ideas of an ever-increasing population, the huge entanglements and multiplications of physical power, swept upon them like a moving thicket, not arisen normally from the earth of experience but preternaturally struck out of the ground.   It was impossible to go back. They had to go forward and to associate with the idea of expiation and redemption the idea of going forward in obedience to numbers and power.   By accepting an obsession, they became enamoured of what they feared.

This is fetichism.   It did not prevent our forefathers from being rationally critical of the means, as distinct from the ends, of their double-revolution.   That its immediate results, in slums, in violence, in criminality, in mechanized commercialism, in debasement of the countryside, in an educational system unmatched with the development of the franchise, were dark and dangerous they saw clearly; and being, as generations go, less callous, less frivolous and abler than most, they laboured earnestly to produce what Tennyson called " schemes and systems " which should make the forward movement easier.   But they shut their minds against the vision, which continually haunted their prophets and sages, of an internal corruption of their endeavours.   They could not carry self-criticism to the point of acknowledging that, because the poison in the veins of society was a corrupt compound of power-thinking with numerical-thinking, all schemes and all systems, however expedient at short-term and however merciful in intention, were self-defeating if they had their origin in the same corruption.   Even less were they able, in an age so

rich in the evidences of genius and so powerful in its intellectual impulses, to carry self-crititism to the point of acknowledging that they were locking themselves out of certain rooms
of their mind and hanging fetichistic labels on the doors.

*The
Twentieth-
century
Disease:
Power
and
Numbers*

This self-criticism we can no longer avoid. That disease
of society which ends in the annihilation of independent
thought, and of the will to independence, is a disease of rare
subtlety which, by causing men to believe that they are
thinking freely when they are not, flatters them and conceals
itself. It is a disease which gives none of the warnings of
pain but insinuates itself by the pleasant temptations of ease
and pride. During the twentieth century its progress has
been so spectacular and so violently accelerated that it has
called attention to itself. The simplest and least analytical
of men are aware of its existence, though not yet of its nature.
They say, with an unamused smile, that " really the world
seems to be going mad; nothing adds up any more "; they
have a profound sense of the irrational, the irresponsible, the
compelled, in human affairs. Not only are they vaguely
aware of the disease and of their becoming less and less masters
in the house of their own minds, but they have had forced
upon them a partial recognition of the two principal sources of
the disease.

The source in power has declared itself, though recognition
of it remains incomplete. The atomic bomb is feared, but as
yet only the bomb. Enough of the fetichistic idea of progress
survives to conceal the truth that the peril of nuclear physics
consists in the disproportion of its power to the wisdom of
mankind and that this disproportion remains whether the
power is used to make a bomb or to drive a machine. Atomic
power is potentially a thousand industrial revolutions com-
pressed into the time-space of a few months. It is not pessimism but common-sense to foresee that its civil uses may
result in an intolerable distortion of life on earth for which

mankind is economically, politically and spiritually unfit. The need to understand and take measures against this threat of civil distortion is as imperative as the need to keep the bomb in its cage. Only the highest and most selfless authority, perhaps American, can bring it home to the mind of the world. Meanwhile it is a sign of hope that the world's mind is less entangled than it was in an association of the idea of power with the idea of beneficent progress, and has become—though still within limits that have to be broken down—questioning and self-critical.

The second source of distress—its source in numerical thinking—is less understood, but even this has begun to declare itself. It is seen as inescapably true that, as votes increase in number, each vote diminishes in effect; the democratic currency is debased. An elector who weighs his choice and honestly tries to make it bear upon long-term policy is discouraged by knowing that his vote is cancellable by any one of millions of votes thoughtlessly cast. Even a vehement party-man or the most frivolous of self-seekers is aware of an extravagant contrast between the intensely personal quality of his needs or his hopes or his hatreds and his electoral resemblance to a grain of sand on a gusty day. By having been pressed to an extreme, the doctrine of numbers has become an incubus of which the burden is felt even by the least discerning. Events external to the English-speaking peoples have brought the numerical development of their democracies into the field of criticism. Abroad, they have seen fully exemplified the old Aristotelean teaching of that cycle of human affairs in which extreme democracy leads to tyranny as certainly as one season follows another. The United States is happily protected by its Constitution. No majority in one house could within a year legally abolish elections, the courts of law, and all the liberties of the people. In England, where this has already been made possible, the destructive cycle is not yet complete, but it is far advanced. Every constitutional barrier against tyranny has been removed. If an effective Second Chamber is not re-created, the Executive has to take but one step to dictatorship. This is beginning to be understood. A reconstructive measure of constitutional and electoral reform is a prime necessity and not so far out of reach as it was.*

Everything, including democracy, is destroyed by its own extremes: personal rule by absolutism; oligarchy, or bureaucracy, by closeness, rigidity and centralization; plutocracy by avarice; democracy by a watering of its only valid currency of self-discipline and self-respect. Each polity is enabled to endure by its acceptance of limitations upon itself. To cast off those limitations is death. An unlimited and numerical democracy follows, with certain local variants, always the same course. First, it loses sight of the truth that the principle of democracy is consent, and that majority-rule, so designed that one majority may be freely substituted for another within a constitutional framework, is not a divine ordinance but a convenient method of giving effect, stage by stage, to a gradual development of a national will. When this truth has been lost sight of, a decaying democracy impatiently casts off those constitutional restraints which are in its body politic what self-discipline is in the life of a man. The majority-for-the-time-being attributes virtue to its own numbers and thinks of those who differ from it not as fellow-men but as parasites and vermin. Governments then arise which, building a doctrine of infallibility upon numbers, repudiate the triple obligation of majority governments: first, their obligation as trustees for the minority; second, their obligation to preserve the constitutional framework within which governments may be checked and replaced; and, finally, their obligation even to their own majority, the representatives of which they treat more and more as a claque and less and less as responsible

* See pages 74–78.

members of a parliamentary assembly.   The same evils appear with even greater virulence where a mob-minority, also associating virtue with power but believing that justice resides not even in the counting of heads but in a quasi-mystical coagulation of the elect, usurps the name of democracy.   In either case, of tyrannical majority or tyrannical minority, the conclusion of the cycle of numerical thinking is always the cretinous stage in which what was once individual judgement becomes a wolfish howling under balconies, and what were once men and women are but a single tongue to lick the hand of a dictator.

There is good reason to believe that distrust of power- *Disease* thinking and of numerical-thinking has grown among the *Partly Under-* Western peoples.   The atom-bomb and the collapse of *stood* democracy in state after state are facts that neither optimism nor indifference has been able to disregard.   But whether those who observe and shrink from these disasters have yet grasped the connexion of both with the liberties of the mind is more open to doubt.   Say to a man: life on earth is threatened with extermination, and he will assent with horror, for the threat is to his body.   Say to him: numerical thinking is destructive of political liberty and leads to concentration camps, and though he may hesitate, for the threat, in the United States and even in England, is not yet knocking at his door, he is more likely to assent than his Victorian ancestors would have been.   But say to him that both power-thinking and numerical-thinking are threats to the liberties of his mind and that only by preserving these liberties can men continue to have the *means* to criticize and so to remedy their ills, and he is likely to shrug his shoulders at too subtle an abstraction. This is a reason for hoping that, in one or other of the ensuing essays, each reader may find his own way towards a central problem, from which, if it were presented only in the form of abstract analysis, he might turn away.

The Power
of Evil:
Evidence
of
Activity

Nevertheless, I should, like Queen Elizabeth, be returning an " answer answerless ", if I were not to say, before ending this introduction, that the problem of the liberty of thought, though it has constitutional and educational and æsthetic aspects which appear in later pages, is in my own view spiritual.

Either there is an immortal part of us or there is not. If there is not, then all argument above the level of comfort and expediency is vain, and we are to think of our lives as we should of a month's stay in a boarding-house if we had no remembrance of any existence before our coming to it or hope of going beyond it. In those conditions behaviour would not necessarily be vicious or selfish; there are reasons of expediency, hardly distinguishable from ethical reasons, for not abusing a companionship though it endure only for a month; therefore, if we drew up rules for the boarding-house we might still try to give its inhabitants their just share of its comforts, and if we painted pictures we might paint them as well as we could according to our lights; but we should not be concerned with the continuity or growth of our own or of our neighbours' selves. If, on the contrary, there is an immortal part of us, called the spirit, whose lodging-place is in our minds, it is our primary concern that our minds be not corrupted or disabled.

By the same argument, if there is in the world, as many not fools have supposed, a force which may be thought of as being at war with the spirit, its chosen battlefield must be the mind, and the body in so far as the body affects the spirit through the mind. And if the Force of Evil may be spoken of in military metaphor as operating in a series of campaigns or as returning to the attack with new weapons, it is reasonable to look for evidence of the attack's having been renewed in the rocking of the human mind under the shock. Such a rocking and confusion is precisely what the evidence of the nineteenth and twentieth centuries suggests. Tennyson was not using empty rhetoric when he spoke of "a mighty wave of evil passing over the world" and of "a last dim battle of the West". The spirit, the relationship of the creature to the Creator, is being attacked through the mind.

Our present sense of being engaged in such a battle is expressed in different ways by different men. To one it seems that the predicament of the Western world, though its parts may be explained, is not as a whole to be accounted for by mistakes of policy. Whatever fault he may find with the action or inaction of statesmen with whom he disagrees, he finds that these errors wear in retrospect an alarming air of having been compelled. Throughout history, it is true, statesmen have moved within limits prescribed by circumstance, but these limits appear to have narrowed and policy to have become less and less an exercise of free will. Of this, the Yalta conference, however its self-defeat may be interpreted, is an outstanding example.

Another will describe a generalized sense of frustration by saying that the tasks which we have to perform, as citizens or as private men, are becoming continuously more difficult, not, he feels, because we are less capable than our ancestors of returning answers and exercising moral choice, but because the questions themselves are becoming less and less comprehensible. Life is increasingly specialized and complex. Each specialization, financial, economic, scientific or administrative, has developed its own language and symbols. Every measure of national or international organization begets, for example, a wilderness of committees, known by initial letters, whose powers, whose composition and whose very names are forgotten by those whose lives they affect. Newspapers, which have often been great elucidators, are in this matter almost powerless. If they were to explain and re-explain this infinite complexity, they would cease to be read, nor is there any generally understood language in which explanation is possible. Yet they cannot omit all reference to these organizations. They report that one has met in Paris, that another has broken up in New York; they do what can be done in a paragraph to summarize a six weeks' discussion between experts; and the huge alphabets of chaos twine like snakes through their columns, letters of power or of impotence masquerading as power. A few specialists can read some of them, but they cannot communicate with other specialists across the boundaries of their specialization. And what is true of international is as true of national problems. Regulations, demands and orders are made by reference-back to orders, demands and regulations to which the recipient has no access, and which, unless he were at the same time an accountant, a lawyer, a parliamentary draughtsman and a seer, would be incomprehensible to him if he had access to them. Many of them have in fact no meaning, or several meanings which cancel out, for they were written by officials who, not knowing what they wished to express, faded into jargon.

Even more perilous is the dispersal of the human intellect at its highest levels. Science, philosophy, history, even poetry, have developed, as it were, radially, away from the notion of universal and communicable knowledge. Even the desire to communicate appears in many instances to have died. Only in the Courts of Law is there a conspicuous and happy exception. A layman may, even here, be baffled sometimes by his ignorance of a technical term, but in general their Lordships' judgements are masterpieces of the lucid and coherent use of a common language. Elsewhere the radii of specialization have grown apart, like the spokes of a wheel that have no felloe to bind them, and from each spoke or radial stem a thousand diverging branches have sprung out. Each branch has its own language, its own symbols, its own despair of synthesis, its own movement towards a fragmentation of the mind. In political organization, in administrative action, in art itself, it is hard not to feel that the essential questions are being asked in ciphers of which the cipher-makers themselves are losing the key.

Those who express in this way their sense that the ship is not answering her helm, like those who insist that policy has become less and less an exercise of free-will, are saying what Tennyson said, but without using the word " evil ".   It is a word which can no longer be avoided.   If men are not spiritual beings, the word is certainly meaningless.   In that case, nothing matters except to vote for more paper-money until the earth disintegrates.   But if they are spiritual beings engaged in spiritual fight, it is important that we should observe the nature of the enemy and recognize that our minds, their integrity, lucidity and freedom, are the object of attack.

The method of attack is familiar in the history of evil. *Evil's Method of Attack: Conceal- ment and Insinuation* Its beginning is to sap resistance.   This we have seen done.

In countries beyond the Iron Curtain a generation has been raised up which is cut off from the history of religious and humane thought.   Few ideas of virtue remain but those which arise from civic conformity, and little understanding that any other notion of virtue has prevailed among men. Discernment of spiritual evil has been made impossible by isolating the human mind, except within an area of conduct prescribed by an ideology of mass, from the comparative means of estimating value.   Qualitative estimate has been made, in the strict sense of the word, unthinkable, for, at the boundaries guarded by collective dogma, thought stops.   In the Western world, corresponding attempts have been made by the falsi- fication of history and the gradual capture of the educative machine to cut man's line of communication with the sources of his imaginative life.   To this process innocent people are induced to contribute by the craven fear of being thought old- fashioned if they do not submit their children and themselves to new witch-doctors.   Materialists who wish to restrict the liberties of the mind derive a great part of their strength from the fact that the effect of superficial education among the Western peoples has been to make them gullible by their terror of being gulled.   Our age has no baser sentimentality than that which will repudiate any faith that may be laughed at, and no falser pride than that of the tremulously experimental whose minds are so " open " that they will not call a lie a lie if it comes to them talking a fashionable jargon and wearing a new dress.   They will ingenuously listen while it is argued that children should be denied access to fairy-tales.   Why? Because, materialists say, they are not " factual " and lead a child into deceptive and fantastic voyages.   The tremulously experimental know, but dare not admit, that the materialists' real motive for withholding fairy-tales is that, although they are not " factual ", they are true with that truth of vision and experience which men pour into legends.   In their accounts of giants and witches and spells and talismans, fairy-tales give warning of the existence of a principle of evil in the world; in their legends of magic, of the use and the abuse of " wishes ", they imply the power and the responsibility of a freely creative imagination; and from these resources of the spirit, from all knowledge of its opportunities and perils, even of its existence, materialists wish to cut men off.

Less direct pressures upon the public mind to restrict the free exercise of the imaginative faculty are perceptible in many quarters.   Some of these pressures, considered separately, appear trivial; some have their origin in no consciously evil intention ; but they are made important by their convergence upon the liberty of thought.

An example is in the use of the cant adjective " escapist ". This word, at first used to describe a falsely romantic and basely commercialized form of art, was twisted and repeated until it came to be contemptuously applied to all fantasy not bitterly satirical, and to romanticism as such.   The result was that works as different in their greatness as *Notre Dame de Paris* or *Mémoires d'Outre-Tombe* or *Far from the Madding Crowd* or *The Lotos-Eaters* or the *Nuits* of Musset or the Nocturnes of Chopin were held up to inclusive derision. The object was to prevent the making of just distinctions between the good and the bad in romantic art, and gradually to exclude from consideration all art not Marxist. Mr. Eliot's legitimate experiments in language were seized upon as an excuse to conduct a strictly partisan purge of language itself aimed at forbidding the use of such words as " lovely " and " beautiful ", and restricting men's vocabulary, and therefore their thought, to the prescribed jargon of materialism. Æsthetic reasons were given for the purge, and often the supporters of it believed that its intention was æsthetic. It appeared to them as a healthy onslaught upon the excesses of romanticism or of sentimentality. But its origins were darker; the forces controlling it have outrun the dilettanti; a movement which was to have purged art of sentimentality and redeemed the proletariat with a new " astringency " has been overwhelmed throughout the Western world by a cult of violence rooted in sadism and the sentimentality of crime. Once more there has been a devil in the wind.

In many departments of contemporary life, where no intention to damage the mind exists, there is often discernible an effect of damage. The films provide an instance chosen for discussion here for the very reason that there is good in them and that they are an instance, too, of the extreme difficulty, wherever masses are concerned, of safeguarding good from perversion. No one denies that there are certain films which have not a disruptive or restrictive but a positively liberating effect upon the mind, and many others which, though not works of art, have at least as good a claim as many books or plays to be put forward as entertainment. Nevertheless because films are, with exceptions, a mass-product as books and plays are not, and because film-going is a habitual and largely un-selective activity as reading or play-going is not in the same degree, films collectively may be, and often are in their effect on immature minds, an influence to prevent the imagination from flowing outward and discovering for itself its own self-renewals.

The damage is done by averaging and habit.   No form of censorship is a remedy for it.   If the young went to films rarely and selectively there would be little harm, but there is bitter and destructive harm in their going—and, indeed, in anyone's going—twice or three times a week to a programme selected for them.   This not chiefly for the reason commonly given that they may learn gangsterism at this source or that when virtue triumphs on the screen it so often does so for the wrong reasons and is crowned with valueless rewards, but because habitual film-going is habitual acceptance of ready-made imagining, designed to require a minimum effort of the receiver.   No kind of fiction so consistently demands so little of its audience.   The evil of its regular use is much less in the corruptive energy of particular exhibitions of violence than in the films' collective, habit-making power to satisfy imagi-native hunger " out of a can " and so to discourage the secret, individual imagination from following its own quarry.   Their effect appears to be either to lull the mind or, if the mind itself is unstable, to induce in it a condition of hysteria: seldom to inspire in it that contributory wonder, that active and creative meditation, which is the effect of genuine works of art not designed, as films ordinarily are, to produce a response esti-mated numerically.   If this were not true, the word " fan " would not have the meaning it now has.   There are " fans " of particular authors and of particular play-actors and actresses, just as there are " fans " of particular film-stars, and there the word means little more than " admirer " with an emotional overtone.   But whereas " play-fan " is a rare word and " book-fan " is non-existent, " film-fan " is applicable to great masses of the population. It implies fanatical and undiscriminating habit. It has almost the servile meaning of " addict ".

The closest resemblance to the effect of habitual film-going on the mind is to be found in the effect of crooners' music upon those whom it pleases. The evil is in the addiction, and in the mind's acceptance of a kind of imaginative dole which would be unacceptable if the imagination were itself employed. The gangster-films are a trouble to magistrates; that is another question. But for a child to pay ninepence and take the *Odyssey* or the Book of Genesis or *Kubla Khan* out of the slot-machine, for him to be told by the sound-track what the damsel played on her dulcimer and to see the milk of paradise poured from a jug, is a suicide of part of himself. It is, precisely, the form of suicide that the Litany prays against—a hardening of heart, a contempt of the Word—which, by possessing the mind with a false image, excludes truth. It is a submission to the powers of evil, which seek to debase the currency of imagination wherever they find it.

But the materialists' attempts to advance this purpose have not, in the West, the support of a one-party police State. They may produce, and have produced, at a low level of propaganda, popular outlines of world-history so crude that no mention of Christianity occurs in them. With subtler use of the collective method, they may so pervert education that children grow into men without knowing what Christmas commemorates. At a higher intellectual level, they may build a logical structure, leading to a conclusion of ethical and spiritual nihilism, upon the Marxist premises that " the social process is the generator of consciousness " and that Truth is " always generated in action, in instinctive organismal response ".*
But they have not yet, in the West, the power to make it criminal to demonstrate the falsity of their premises : a falsity

* CHRISTOPHER CAUDWELL: *Further Studies in a Dying Culture.*

which appears, logically, in the opposite argument that consciousness is antecedent to society, and Being antecedent to consciousness, and creation antecedent to Being. Upon this order, the responsibility of the human person rests. To destroy that acceptance of it which, from the beginning of time, has been the root of religion and poetry, of fear and love, of self-consciousness and self-knowledge, is to disarticulate the structure of the mind and to make reasonless the reason from which distinctions proceed. The distinction upon which all distinguishing depends is that between the principles of Good and Evil, called, in its intuitive forms, conscience. Dialectical materialism is a technique designed to rub it out, but its complete rubbing out cannot be accomplished while the Gospels and Milton and Bunyan remain accessible, and men are free to pray and love.

In the West, therefore, the windows through which the enemy's approach is visible are not yet shuttered and barred, but the bars and shutters are prepared. Much has already been done to persuade men that to look out of these windows is superstitious and that what the eyes of their vision tell them they see is hallucination. If, as children, they fall into the grip of a teacher who believes that men are a concretion of economic and sexual appetites, they are taught that there is for them something humiliating, something inconsistent with their claim to numerical infallibility, in an admission that there are realities that pass their own and all mankind's understanding. Of these realities love, as distinct from appetite, is one, and evil is another. It is evidently a helpful preliminary to attack upon the soul of man to persuade him that neither exists. And persuasion has gone far.

The Purpose of Attack: Chaos   The purpose of the attack is the old one: to produce chaos. But since the beginning of the nineteenth century, the vulnerability of the human race has been changed. In the past, each man was vulnerable in his own heart; now men are vulnerable also in their collectivity. If the materialists had their way, we should be one Faust, one Œdipus, one Iscariot; there would be, in effect, one collective mind to be possessed. It is as though Satan, in his dark campaigns, finding that each man, while aware of himself as spirit, might retire upon his place of sanctuary and be reborn, had at last found a way to deprive him of this awareness. The chaos to be produced is not material chaos only, for wars and economic confusion are but means to a more dreadful end. The victory aimed at is an ultimate chaos of the world-mind, insanity by the failure of distinctions and the fantasies of power, a blur of fragmented reason in a spinning, causeless, faithless and ungovernable dust.

This victory cannot be achieved as long as the liberties of *The Core of Defence* the mind survive, for it is inconsistent with them. The greatest source of danger is in man's failure to recognize that they, and not the overt liberties only, are being attacked, and that the means of attack, as the Soviet trials and my American friend's visit suggest, are becoming increasingly direct. The purpose of the present book is to assist recognition of the nature of the attack, dating from the early nineteenth century and now reaching its climax, upon those mental and spiritual freedoms which are the breath of reason and faith. The battle to be fought is not between party and party or even, at root, between those whose emphasis is upon faith and those whose emphasis is upon reason. It is rather, as I see it, a struggle, transcending all differences but one, for the validity of the human mind, its right to distinguish between good and evil, and its power to make journeys in the light of that distinction. Faith and reason are companions on an infinite journey. There are no limits, except in our human capacity, to the extension of either. If one of the companions says: " I can go no farther," it is not desertion but courage in the other to go forward alone. Our peril is that there are great forces operating in the world which would forbid the journey and destroy our will to make it, so that it may never more be said that

> News from a foreign country came
> As if my treasure and my wealth lay there.

II. PRINCIPLES

THE LIBERTY OF THOUGHT
THE ARTIST IN THE COMMUNITY

THE LIBERTY OF THOUGHT *

Pour qu'on ne puisse abuser du pouvoir, il faut que,
par la disposition des choses, le pouvoir arrête le pouvoir.
MONTESQUIEU.   *De l'Esprit des Lois, XI. 4.*

THERE are periods in history when the ground upon which
thought has been moving falls apart and a chasm opens in the
mind of the world.   What distinguishes these great divisions
of thought from mere rifts in opinion is that they seem, in
the historical view, always to demand a choice between two
opposed concepts of personality.   They are concerned not
only with how men behave but with what man is.   When
that issue is raised in a new form, a chasm opens; and such a
chasm has, I think, been opening at our feet.

I propose to consider it in terms of the liberty of thought,
and I am not using the phrase as a synonym for the liberty of
expression.   I mean by it the mind's freedom from any
external pressure designed to drug, intimidate or otherwise
reduce its full exercise of natural capacity.   My chief purpose
will be to disengage the liberty of thought from those liberties
of which it has hitherto seemed to be but a constituent part,
and to present it as a distinct liberty cognizable at law.

The cleavage in the world's mind, as I understand it, is no
longer the old one, which statesmanship and law already
recognize, between those who wish to extend and those who
wish to restrict the overt liberties: the liberty of the person,
for example, against imprisonment without trial, or the liberties
of writing and speech.   All these are still in question, but,
whereas in the past they alone have been challenged and the

* Originally entitled: THE LIBERTY OF THOUGHT AND THE SEPARA-
TION OF POWERS: A Modern Problem considered in the context of
Montesquieu.   The Zaharoff Lecture delivered at Oxford, 1948.

liberty of thought has been considered only in its expressions through them, now the liberty of thought itself is directly attacked.

The attack is based upon a mechanistic view of personality in which man appears neither as a spiritual being nor even as an animal having effective volition, but as the instrument of material forces external to him. For those who hold this view the liberty of thought is necessarily a contradiction of their notion of what man is; it is for them a heresy to be extirpated; and this gives a new and fanatical inhumanity to their despotisms. Other despotisms have aimed at the restriction of conduct, but the mechanistic theory and practice aim at destroying liberty by destroying man's will and capacity for it. If Liberty may be spoken of as a river, then it becomes true to say that, whereas in the past those who have taken a Christian or a humane view of man have assumed that the upper reaches of the river were inaccessible to attack, they have now to look to the source.

This development in the controversy of freedom I wish to examine in the context of Montesquieu.

2

Why of Montesquieu? I shall burden you neither with his biography nor with a formal commentary on his work, but as there may be some for whom the *Esprit des lois* is not a bedside book, I shall be forgiven for saying that its author was born in January of the significant year 1689.

Charles Louis de Secondat, who inherited the barony of Montesquieu from his uncle, and who, by virtue of his mother, ran English and Gascon blood in his veins, had in him that admixture of seriousness and gaiety, of love of solitude and love of company, which sometimes makes a dilettante, but endowed him with a remarkably independent greatness.

Having made himself famous in his early thirties by his dashing and satirical *Lettres persanes*, he explored a different area of his genius.   Unlike the greater part of his fellow countrymen, he boldly accepted the culinary risk of leaving France and travelled much abroad.   Again unlike the greater part of his fellow countrymen, he acquired not only an admiration for English institutions but an enduring love of our people and our gardens.   Back in France, he settled down to write his *Considérations sur les causes de la grandeur et de la décadence des Romains*, which, when it appeared in 1734, was frowned upon by the fashionable cliques, who could not see it as a forerunner, almost a preliminary sketch, of his masterpiece. The *Esprit des lois* itself was published in 1748.

Montesquieu, after enjoying its triumph, had the good fortune to die in 1755, leaving it to Burke and Burke's opponents to decide whether he would have been the first of the *émigrés* or have thrown up his cap for the Revolution.   He was exempted from that embarrassing choice, for when Louis XVI summoned the States General and Liberty prepared to take the bit between her teeth, Montesquieu, more blessed in this than many reformers, had attained the refuge of Saint-Sulpice with the comfortable margin of over forty years.   Given the conditions of his nature—aristocracy without more than a just pride, Christianity without fanaticism, and liberalism without any enduring equalitarian delusions—no one could have chosen better than he the place and period of his tenure of this earth.   *La douceur de vivre*—which I dare to translate as the sweetness of being intelligently alive!   Paris and Bordeaux: 1689–1755!   To have lived there, to have lived then; to have been capable of French prose and of European thought; to have written an enduring masterpiece in a study as long as a cricket-pitch and proportionately wide, and to have had servants who cleaned it and fuel that warmed it; to have left Bordeaux for ever four years earlier than Marat's arrival there

to study medicine; to have made your exit from this world
three years before Robespierre entered it and within three
days of Talleyrand's becoming one year old—what a triumph
of discreet chronology!

3

It may still be asked why the thirty-one books of the *Esprit
des lois*, sprung from the vanished world of pre-revolutionary
France, should be revived now.

A work of political philosophy lives in proportion to its
power to compel men to re-think it.   The supreme works in
this kind, the *Politics* of Aristotle, for example, are always
being re-thought.   Below, but not far below, the Aristotelian
level are a few other works of political philosophy which,
though they have not the timeless universality of the *Politics*,
are not only landmarks in the development of European ideas
but have the quality of self-renewal.   It would be childish
to say that they go out of date; they are always relevant, but
sometimes they seem to be a little way removed from our
preoccupations, and we neglect them.   Then new threats to
liberty appear, new enemies of reason, new challenges to
faith; and these books re-emerge in answer to our present
necessities.

The *Esprit des lois* emerges in this way.   Its special claim
upon us is one that may, at the moment, seem paradoxical:
it envisages despotism but not what we mean by totalitarianism, and is, therefore, primarily concerned with the overt
liberties; but this enables us to make a valuable distinction
to which we might not otherwise have been led.   Though
Montesquieu, except in a single paragraph,* omitted from his
consideration the liberty of thought as the separate and vulnerable liberty that it is become to-day, he has left room for it.
His system, when re-examined, is seen to include and converge

* *E.L.* xii. 11.

THE LIBERTY OF THOUGHT

upon it.   It is almost as if, in writing the *Esprit des lois*, he had left certain blank pages on which the twentieth century might set out its tragic history without disturbing the coherence of his book.

4

Let us now re-think his idea of liberty, and particularly of democratic liberty and probity.

" Philosophic liberty ", he says, " consists in the exercise of one's will, or at least (if we must speak agreeably to all systems) in the opinion that one exercises it." *   Again he says: " Liberty can consist only in the power of doing what we ought to will, and in not being constrained to do what we ought not to will." †   At once, in the phrase ' what we ought to will '—*ce que l'on doit vouloir*—he indicates his recognition of an ultimate moral sanction of all law and of the reality of human volition.   His opposition to the mechanistic view appears instantly.

But Montesquieu was not an abstract philosopher.   His method was to observe the world around him and the world as it had been, and to draw certain practical conclusions on the subject of liberty.   In the course of these investigations he discerned different types of government, each with a principle or actuating force proper to it, and two divisions of liberty: the constitutional and the personal.   He proceeded to relate all these to one another.   Our immediate concern is with Montesquieu's democracy and Montesquieu's despotism. These we must re-think.

" The principle of despotic government ", he says, " is fear."‡ This is familiar enough.   But Montesquieu's despotisms—for he was an eager orientalist—were generally associated in his mind, except when he was thinking of Sparta, with the softening influences of the seraglio.   They were indolent, they were

---

* *E.L.* xii. 2.   † *E.L.* xi. 3.   ‡ *E.L.* v. 14.

capricious; ours are systematic.   His were, in many things,
particularly in their attitude towards men's private lives,
tolerant.   They restricted those actions of individuals which
were offensive to the despot, but it was not part of their theory
to annihilate individuality itself.

Montesquieu's democracy is defined as a government in
which the body of the people has supreme power.   Its principle or actuating force is, he says, " virtue ",* and he makes
it clear † that he means by this " political virtue " or probity.
It is the antithesis of political corruption in all its forms, of
the people as well as of the government.

He is very illuminating on the subject, and, as always, compassionate for human weakness.   Probity is not easy.   It is
not to be had by preaching and threats.   If we want a people
to be honest we must not so oppress them with taxation that
honesty becomes the worst policy.‡   We must not legislate
against the grain, for, says Montesquieu, " it is very bad policy
to change by laws what ought to be changed by customs ";§
nor must we exasperate men by constant interference with
" la conduite intérieure ".   There is, he reminds us, a form of
tyranny which, though it does not arise from direct oppression,
" is seated in opinion and is sure to be felt whenever those who
govern establish things shocking to the turn of thought of a
nation—des choses qui choquent la manière de penser d'une
nation ". ‖   La conduite intérieure . . . la manière de penser . . .
it is clear in what direction Montesquieu's thought is running.

One of the dangers of over-legislating and of pestering
people in their private lives is that the law itself, without which
there can be neither liberty nor probity, may be brought into
ridicule and contempt.   " When, in a popular government,"
Montesquieu says, " there is a suspension of the laws, as this
can proceed only from the corruption of the republic, the state

* E.L. iii. 3.   † In his Défense de l'Esprit des lois.
‡ E.L. xiii. 1.   § E.L. xix. 14.   ‖ E.L. xix. 3.

is certainly undone." * He means that the laws may become inoperative because the public has ceased to regard them. Laws may become so many, so confusing, so impossible to obey, that ordinary citizens shrug their shoulders and put the forms into the waste-paper basket. Probity ceases to be valued because it has been made impracticable. The result is described by Montesquieu with terrible force. " When probity is banished," he says, ". . . avarice possesses the whole community. Desires now change their objects; what men cared for once, they care for no longer; they were free within the laws, they will now be free against the laws." * Our word for this is the black market. . . . Montesquieu continues : " Not greed but frugality is now called avarice ", and I hear a voice, I hear a thousand thousand voices cry out : " What is the good of saving? Savings are capital. They will all be taken from you ! " . . . But I continue to quote Montesquieu : " Formerly ", he says, " the wealth of individuals was the public treasure, but now the public treasure is paid out to private persons. *La république est une dépouille* "—I must, with your permission, translate freely—" The state is despoiled, the state is a pigeon, and its strength is no longer anything but the power of some citizens and the licentiousness of all." * Let us leave it there.

From Montesquieu's vast survey three governing ideas emerge : the idea of relativity; the idea of balance; and the idea of the Rule of Law.

The whole scheme of his book, which considers laws in their relationship to climate, to soil, to morals, to population, declares his idea of relativity. The *Esprit des lois* is an essay, not on the looseness but on the science of toleration. And as, when he considered personal liberty, he looked into men's homes and asked what laws would suit their differences, so when he considered political or constitutional liberty, he

* *E.L.* iii. 3.

looked first into men's minds. " Political liberty in a man ",
he said, " is——" What do you think? Conservatism?
Liberalism? Socialism? Communism? " Political liberty
in a man ", he said, " is that peace of mind which arises from
his sense of his own safety." * That peace of mind! *Cette
tranquillité d'esprit!* . . . Who has it? *La tranquillité d'esprit* is
not far removed from *la liberté de pensée.* Montesquieu con-
verges on our subject. Everywhere he rejects the conception
of man as an instrument without effective will or immortal
spirit, and in his *Défense* he repudiates with energy and passion
the idea of a blind fate, *une fatalité aveugle.*†

Looking back at this stage of our argument, and asking what
meaning, consistent with Montesquieu's teaching, may be
given to liberty in the free societies of the West, we might, I
think, return such an answer as this:

A man's liberty is that area of his life in which his individuality moves freely. It is finite, unless we speak mystically of
his union with the Infinite. In all other senses, political or
personal, objective or subjective, his liberty is restricted, is
defined and secured by its restrictions, and is not to be thought
of except in terms of them. As a room is not a room that
has no walls, so liberty is not liberty that has no boundaries.
It is an area, not space.

Its value, like a room's, does not depend on its size only.
It depends on its interior beauty, its proportion, its light and
warmth, its outlook, the use that is made of it; on its quiet
sometimes, and sometimes on the company received there;
always on a man's knowledge that it is his, and that, when he
goes out, it will await his coming back. The room has this
special quality: that it is not his residence only, but his home.
Drive him from it, surrender it to the habitation of alien spirits,

* *E.L.* xi. 6.

† See HAZARD, PAUL, *La Pensée européenne au XVIIIᵉ siècle*, Paris,
Boivin, 1946, ii, pp. 99–106, where the author sees in Montesquieu's
theological position " *un embarras dont il n'est jamais sorti* ".

and he is a homeless one, a wanderer in the desert of existence, where the shapes of loneliness pursue him by day and by night, and his breath is fear.   The room is his home, where love nourished and experience taught him, where he is capable of innocence and renewal; it is the origin of his courage to issue out, the hope of his return and his redemption.   This room looks for its glory to three things: his vision and its ghosts; his sense of peace in it; his assurance that it is not a prison. It is no liberty to dwell in terror of being invaded.   It is no liberty to ring for a banquet if it be a jailer who carries in the tray.

But it is liberty to know oneself; and by transcendence of knowledge to be oneself; and by penetration of being to lose oneself; and, in losing, find.

5

Turn aside now from liberty.   These are Marx's words: "The phantasmagorias in the human brain are enforced supplements of man's material vital process.   Morality, religion, metaphysics and ideology in general, with their appropriate forms of consciousness, thus forfeit the semblance of independence." *   And he adds: "Consciousness does not determine life."

Consider another passage.   "The necessaries of life", says Marx, "are, above all, food, drink, shelter, clothing and a few others.   Hence, the first historical act is the production of the means for the satisfaction of these needs, and this one historical act is the fundamental determinant of all history.   What individuals are coincides with what they produce; and not only with what they produce but with how they produce." †

If we should ask whether the production of the means was

* MARX, *German Ideology*, Int. Pub. N.Y., p. 24.   Quoted by SCHWARZSCHILD, L., *The Red Prussian*, London, Hamilton, 1947.

† *Ibid.*, p. 7.

not necessarily preceded by two volitional processes—that which distinguished the need as a need and placed it in an order of needs, and that which imagined, chose, and devised the means of satisfying it—Marx gives the answer we are waiting for in his letter to P. V. Annenkov of 28 December 1846. Having elsewhere declared that the productive forces are the sole determinant of history, he says now: " Men are not free to choose their own productive forces."

This emphasizes the distinction which I wish to make. Marxism is rooted in an absolute denial that there has ever been, or can ever be, effective human volition.   Even the proletariat is, in Marx's words, " the material weapon of philosophy ",* and by " philosophy " he meant precisely what Montesquieu passionately repudiated: *une fatalité aveugle.*

6

I turn back now to Montesquieu with the object of applying his warnings and safeguards.

It is evident that the Mechanists of today are using two methods: the suppression of overt liberties among peoples within reach of their armed forces, and the discouraging of the idea of liberty among peoples more distant.   It is against the inward corruption of liberty that Montesquieu's warnings are issued.

A principal sign of it is a respect for uniformity.   There are, Montesquieu says, certain ideas of uniformity " which infallibly appeal to little minds.   They find in them a kind of perfection." †

An uncritical desire for uniformity is a step towards that abdication of choice which Mechanists require men to make. No class, particularly in England since the Industrial Revolu-

---

* MARX-ENGELS, *Gesamt-Ausgabe*, Abteilung I, Band 1, Halb-Band 1, pp. 619–20.   Quoted by Schwarzschild, p. 86.
  † *E.L.* xxix. 18.

tion, has been free of this tendency.   Now, enforced by the drabness of our conditions and the disastrous overcrowding of our schools, uniformity has become a menace to the use of reason and the exercise of free will.   " When you train an animal ", says Montesquieu, " you take good care not to let him change his master, his lesson or his pace.   You strike his brain with two or three movements, and no more. . . . *Vous frappez son cerveau par deux ou trois mouvements, et pas davantage.*" *   The means of striking the brain with two or three movements are more powerful than they were in Montesquieu's time.   They may be employed, as never before, against the mind itself.   Let us beware of them when they come bearing the gifts of cheapness, of entertainment, of instruction, of expediency.   They may have these advantages. Let us still beware how, under the guise of official patronage or subsidy or the discriminatory allocation of paper, our books, our theatres, our pictures, our very thoughts, are chosen for us.   Education and true leisure enable men to exercise judgement; propaganda and mass-entertainment persuade them to surrender it.

Montesquieu issues other warnings that it may be convenient for us to re-think.   He was well aware that, altogether apart from the frontal attacks which tyrants deliver when the time is ripe, there are mining operations which, among naturally easy-going people, may pass unobserved.   What are these mining operations?   By what signs are we to know that they are going on?   By a government's ill-manners, Montesquieu suggests with the humane wisdom that is characteristic of him, or by the tendency of a majority, in the moment of its success, to tread down a defeated minority.   " Under pretence of establishing the republic's cause ", he says, " they (the triumphant ones) establish a tyranny of vengeance." †   Nor must Ministers be allowed to identify themselves with the

* *E.L.* v. 14.   † *E.L.* xii. 18.

Sovereign and treat attacks upon themselves as equivalent to the crime of *lèse-majesté*.* Moreover, officialdom must be accessible. "The Czar Peter I", Montesquieu reminds us, "has published an edict by which he forbids any of his subjects to offer him a petition until two"—it seems that then only duplicates were required—"until two have been presented to his officers. On refusal of justice, they may present him with a third, but on pain of death if they are wrong. Since then no one has addressed a petition to the Czar." †

"Since then no one has addressed a petition to the Czar"! It is this dulled acquiescence that Montesquieu dreads. How much easier it is to see injustice done than to go to the Courts for protection against jacks-in-office! How flattering it is to our instinct for moderation to keep company with those everlasting and tepid twins, On-the-One-Hand and On-the-Other, whose counsel is always to let a principle go by default! All those warnings which we have hitherto considered may have been given, and given repeatedly, and still the modest and conciliatory may say: "But are there not other explanations of this or this or this than a betrayal of liberty?" They may long hesitate, and rightly hesitate, to cry: "Liberty is in danger! The issue of conscience is raised! Here, at all costs, I stand!" Nevertheless the time may come—the time may already have come—when the Western nations must vindicate their own principle of freedom, and, together and severally, set their house in order. For that purpose, not only may they have to resist new attempts to undermine their fortress; they may have, by great measures of alliance abroad and of repeal and codification at home, to undo harm already done. What is the final and unmistakable signal of that necessity?

* *E.L.* xii. 8.   † *E.L.* xii. 26.

7

Montesquieu's answer is clear: the concentration of powers in one set of hands. Personal liberty cannot survive without constitutional liberty, and for Montesquieu constitutional liberty rests upon that doctrine of his which is called the Separation of Powers.

It is this doctrine that we are called upon to re-think. It was not Montesquieu's invention.* His greatness, as Professor Dedieu has shown, consists in his having produced an orderly analysis and synthesis from the chaos of political theory which, in spite of Locke and Puffendorf, had bemused Europe since the death of Louis XIV. He based his system on a particular example, that of England, whose constitution he called a mirror of liberty, and then proceeded to a series of masterly generalizations.

It has often been objected that his observation of the English constitution was inaccurate. The weight of the charge against him is that, coming to England in 1729 in the midst of Walpole's administration, he believed that the executive and legislative powers were more distinct than in fact they were, and that he failed to understand in what way the Cabinet system was developing. Such ignorance, in a friend of Bolingbroke, is, on the face of it, improbable, but the legend of Montesquieu's inaccuracy dies hard.

The reason is not far to seek. It was once accepted as a truism of our historical studies that the evolution of the Cabinet worked for liberty because the Cabinet, being responsible to Parliament, was an effective check upon the monarch. Dr. Trevelyan's grace and authority made us all familiar with this theory, and he rubbed it in with a devastating footnote at

* See for the ancestry of Montesquieu's ideas, DEDIEU, J., *Montesquieu*, Paris, Alcan, 1913; and, particularly for their English sources, DEDIEU, J., *Montesquieu et la tradition politique anglaise en France*, Paris, Lecoffre, 1909.

Montesquieu's expense. "The English in those days", he said, "were better politicians than political theorists. They permitted the French philosopher, Montesquieu, to report to the world in his *Esprit des lois* that the secret of British freedom was the separation of executive and legislative, whereas the opposite was much nearer the truth." * One does not, except with reluctance and great respect, dissent from the Master of Trinity, but I dare to wonder whether that footnote is not a little too brusquely English or too emphatically Whig. I seem to hear in it the tone of an ancestral voice, speaking on the same subject. "The English at that time", wrote Macaulay, "considered a Frenchman who talked about constitutional checks and fundamental laws as a prodigy not less astonishing than the learned pig or the musical infant."

In any case, is Dr. Trevelyan's footnote justified? It is true that the movement of the executive power, embodied in Walpole and his associates, away from the monarch into the Legislature, was a movement away from separation, and it is true that, *as long as the danger of despotism lay in the monarch*, this movement was a valuable check; and this, of course, was Dr. Trevelyan's point. But the danger no longer lies where it lay in the eighteenth century. Would he not, having regard for what has happened constitutionally since that footnote was written, give Montesquieu credit for long sight?

I cannot help thinking that Montesquieu would have been better understood if his ruling doctrine had been called, not the Separation of Powers, but the Balance of Powers. "To prevent the abuse of power", he says, "it is necessary that, by the disposition of things, power check power ... *il faut que, par la disposition des choses, le pouvoir arrête le pouvoir*." † That, and not separation pedantically insisted upon, is the heart of his teaching.

---

* TREVELYAN, G. M., *History of England*, London, Longmans, 1926, p. 511, footnote.   † *E.L.* xi. 4.

It is as an advocate of balance and check that Montesquieu has always been interpreted by wise and practical men. The fathers of the United States constitution had a much more formal respect for the Separation of Powers than the English ever had.* They spoke of Montesquieu as " the oracle who is always consulted on ... this invaluable precept in the science of politics ", and yet Madison, in the number of *The Federalist* which contains these words, was careful to point out that rigid separation was impracticable, and that in fact Montesquieu, having the English constitution in mind, could not have intended any such stiffness.† What matters is the balance and check arising from a degree of separation. Upon this contention the United States constitution was built and in this sense the Supreme Court appears to have steadily interpreted it, guided always by two complementary principles: that the Executive and the Legislature must never be identified, and that the extent to which they may, in varying circumstances, be allowed to overlap is to be determined, not by considerations either of pedantry or of expediency, but by asking whether, by the degree of overlap, the constitution is or is not being subverted.‡

* It was again and again written into the constitutions of the several States before the Revolution, and, when the time came to federate, the authors of that policy had the Separation of Powers continually in their minds. See SWISHER, C. B., *The Growth of Constitutional Power in the United States*, Chicago, University Press, 1946, particularly pp. 19–20.

† Having shown how often, in England, the powers overlap, Madison quotes Montesquieu and continues: " It may be clearly inferred that ... he did not mean that these departments ought to have no *partial* agency in, or no *control* over, the acts of each other ", but " that where the *whole* power of one department is exercised by the same hands which possess the *whole* power of another department, the fundamental principles of a free constitution are subverted." *The Federalist*, no. 47, 1 February 1788. The italics are Madison's.

‡ In *The Panama Refining Company* v. *Ryan*, commonly known as the *Hot Oils Case* of 1934, the Court set aside an act of Congress on the ground of its violating a maxim that " the Legislature may not delegate its powers "; but if this be read in conjunction with the Court's ruling in *United States* v. *Curtiss-Wright Export Corporation* [1936], and in the

The English, whose constitution is unwritten, have, according to their empirical lights and with battles and vicissitudes well illustrated by the cases of Wilkes and Lord Ellenborough, pursued the same complementary principles, but, as it must seem to any logical American, strangely at haphazard. As a result there is a long list of exceptions which we allow to the principle of the Separation of Powers, and yet the principle is not dead. But we have reason to be anxious for its health. Its death *is* totalitarianism.

It has remained alive, particularly as regards the Judiciary, because the Executive, though it appoints, cannot dismiss Judges, and because a doctrine which, if I may coin a phrase, I would call the doctrine of Distinct Capacities has, throughout our English life, been believed in and, for the most part, honourably observed. My fallible friend may be, in another capacity, my trusted doctor; my wildly talkative guest may yet, as my lawyer, be the impenetrable guardian of my confidence. So may a Lord Chancellor, as a member of the government, be for me a political opponent from whose opinions and tastes I vigorously dissent, and yet, when he puts off his politics and puts on his judgeship, I am, and know that I am, secure of justice. The Executive is based upon faction and it appoints Judges; but the doctrine of Distinct Capacities is observed; it does not factiously appoint Judges. A Judge, in his turn, may be a party man, but it is not as a party man that he interprets the law. This recognition by us of distinct capacities in the same man, and by the same man in himself, is of profound importance. It is the oil which enables the Separation of Powers to work. If it were to decay, if the

---

light of the evident fact that Congress does delegate powers " cognate to " the powers of the President, and did so with conspicuous generosity in the Lease Lend Act, these complementary principles clearly emerge. See CORWIN, E. S., *The Constitution and What it Means Today*, 9th ed., Princeton, 1947, pp. 110–14. Also the same author's *The President : Office and Powers*, New York, University Press, 1941.

overlap of powers were abused, the free conduct of public life would become impossible.

This danger seems comfortably remote from us. Whatever else in the body politic may be corrupt, the High Court, we say rightly, is not. Our danger is not for that reason negligible. The incorruption of the Courts is of little avail if the subject is denied the right of appeal to them from the ruling of a Minister or of his subordinate. The incorruption of the Courts is of little avail if executive regulations having the force of law are so many,* so often changed, and so loosely drawn, that their effect depends less upon their definition of an offence than upon an almost limitless discretion in a prosecutor. Again, the incorruption of the Courts is of little avail if they are called upon to administer laws so vague and unknowable as to force upon Judges an exercise of mere opinion that does not properly belong to the judicial function. Judgements, says Montesquieu, ought to be fixed, " and to such a degree that they are an exact rendering of the law. If they were the private opinion of the Judge, we should live in society without knowing precisely what obligations it laid us under." †

* The Lord Chief Justice, giving judgement in *Harding* v. *Price*, said that " in these days, when offences were multiplied by regulations and orders to an extent which made it difficult for the most law-abiding subjects to avoid offending against the law, it was more important than ever to adhere to the principle (see *Brend* v. *Wood*, [1946], T.L.R. 462, p. 463) that, unless a statute clearly ruled out *mens rea* as a constituent part of a crime, the Court should not find a man guilty of an offence against the criminal law unless he had a guilty mind ". *The Times*, 31 January 1948.

† *E.L.* xi. 6. Montesquieu points out, in many connexions, the opportunities given to tyranny by unascertainable laws. The rule applies to finance. Ministers, he says (xiii. 1), often levy taxes to satisfy their own crankiness, " *une certaine impuissance d'esprit contre les fantaisies* ". Eastern despots, being fortunately indolent, are less given to this vice than Ministers of moderate governments. " The governors of the state ", he says, " do not torment it because they do not perpetually torment themselves. But, as for us, it is impossible that we should ever have any order in our finances because we always know that we shall have something or other to do without ever knowing what it will be." *E.L.* xiii. 15.

Our Courts are not corrupt; they are not instruments of the Executive; but there is an evident and increasing danger that, *par la disposition des choses*, the balance of the constitution may be tipped farther and farther against the Judiciary, and the subject be deprived of the protection it once gave him against private and public tyranny.

8

Whether this fate awaits us or not depends upon the answer given by us and by all the Western nations to the yet larger question: is a democracy, based upon a universal franchise, able and willing to perform those acts of self-discipline and self-restraint which alone can enable it to preserve its liberty? Montesquieu puts this question in concrete form: will democracy preserve the Balance of Powers? Unchecked power is no less tyranny because someone has voted for it.

In countries with a written constitution the removal of checks upon power is blessedly difficult. The people of the United States have wisely denied themselves the opportunity to sweep away their institutions and plunge themselves into slavery by the impulse of one vote. In England we are able, if we will, to destroy, with appalling rapidity, every check upon the exercise of absolute power. It is clearly not understood in the country, or even by sections of the House of Commons itself, to what an extent, by concentrating power in a simple majority of one House, we have laid ourselves open, in some moment of hysteria or intimidation, to a *coup d'état*.

Montesquieu's warning is plain and direct. First, he shows us upon what, in his day, our liberties depended. " Here then ", he says, " is the fundamental constitution of the government of which we speak. The legislative body being composed of two parts, one checks the other by the mutual privilege of rejecting. They are both bound by the executive power as the executive is by the legislative." * What has happened to these checks? Since 1911, the Upper House has had no power finally to reject any measure approved by the Lower. That check is gone, though a brief delaying-power remains. Again, Montesquieu says that the Legislature is checked by the Executive; he is thinking of the monarch's power to withhold the Royal Assent; but this power is now exercised upon the advice of Ministers; that check also is gone. Nothing at all remains to prevent a simple majority in the Lower House from doing whatever passion may suggest or fear compel. It may, after brief delay, abolish general elections, vote itself into permanent power, repeal every statute protective of liberty, and set up a totalitarian state. All this may now be done legally and without a revolutionary act. The opportunity given to plotters is unparalleled.

The truth of this is undiminished by two facts which may, for a moment, appear to contradict it: the first, that Bills to prolong the life of Parliament beyond five years were excluded from the operation of the Parliament Act of 1911; the second, that this exclusion survived the Parliament Act of 1949. The original power of the House of Lords to throw out such Bills is thus maintained and may seem to provide a safeguard against any ambition of a majority in the Lower House to perpetuate itself.

But the supposed safeguard is unreal. Under the Act of 1949, the House of Commons can, within a year, force through a third Parliament Act depriving the House of Lords of this safeguarding power; and if the third Parliament Act, like that of 1949, were made retrospective, and if a Bill to abolish elections had been introduced at the same time with it, elections would be legally abolished without further delay as soon as the third Parliament Act became law.

It is, therefore, true, though few understand it to be so,

* *E.L.* xi. 6.

that whoever can command for one year a majority in the House of Commons can without illegality subvert the Courts, cause parliaments to cease, and establish himself in absolute power. Thus to lay open the path to totalitarian ambition was probably not the intention of many who voted for the Parliament Acts, but it has been the effect of their action. There is, in consequence, urgent need of a new Act redefining the composition and powers of the Second Chamber, and it is a principle essential to such an Act that the Second Chamber shall not depend for its existence or for all its powers either upon the will of the First Chamber acting alone or upon the advice which the Executive may give to His Majesty. In the Second Chamber, once it has been made predominantly non-hereditary, must reside a part of that Sovereignty which is the Sovereignty of " The King in Parliament ".

This is not to suggest that the Second Chamber, any more than the First, should be invested with a power apart from and independent of the electorate. A reconstituted Second Chamber would itself be in great part elective, though it might not be, and ought not to be, elected on the same basis as the First Chamber. If the Second Chamber should differ in opinion from the First, the electors would be arbiters of that difference and would give effect to their will by electing to the Second Chamber (though perhaps not all at the same moment) men who shared their opinions. That electoral change in the Second Chamber should be less abrupt than electoral change in the First and take place at different times is a common-sense expedient which we might well borrow, with modifications, from the U.S. constitution.

The whole question is how best to ensure that the considered will of the people shall prevail and that they shall always be free to revise their decisions. Some hold the view that this can best be done by restoring the suspensory veto of the Second Chamber to a period which would in practice compel the Government of the day to refer a disputed issue back to the people in a General Election. From this view I dissent for three reasons: (1) that it is dangerous constitutionally to give the Second Chamber power to compel a dissolution of the First; (2) that the forcing of a General Election might be unpopular in itself, and lead to confusion of the issue; and (3) that if the forced dissolution occurred early in a Parliament, it might in effect be a reference back to an ephemeral mood which had recently elected the Commons.

What must prevail in great matters is not a particular mood of the people but their persistent and considering will, and I submit that this object would be better attained by requiring of the people that they re-elect a proportion of the Second Chamber periodically and in giving to the Second Chamber meanwhile a firm veto over Bills not certified as Finance Bills, than by referring specific issues to the verdict of a " snap " General Election.*

Whatever balance is struck, a new balance must certainly be found in Great Britain. The present unbalance is too perilous to liberty. By concentrating power in the Lower House; by removing the check once provided by the Upper; by arming the Cabinet with the Royal Prerogative and, when Orders in Council are considered, with extensions of that Prerogative that would have shocked James II; by thus flouting every principle of balance for which Montesquieu stood and upon which our own Revolution Settlement was based, we have paved the way that leads from Moscow to Prague and from Prague to London. It is time that Liberty rebuilt her barricades.

The too comfortable answer is that, though the House of Commons has power to commit these excesses, it has no intention of committing them. In view of the condition of the

* The six preceding paragraphs were added after the passage of the Parliament Act of 1949.

world, is that a reason for abandoning every safeguard? To create a Trust does not imply a belief that the beneficiaries intend to ruin themselves and their heirs; only a determination that they shall not. *Il faut que le pouvoir arrête le pouvoir.* Our surviving liberties, such as they are, depend upon· a fashion in velvet gloves, and they are wearing thin.

Once more, Montesquieu's warning is unmistakable. It is addressed to England; it is applicable to all countries still free. "As all things human", he says, "have an end, the state of which we speak will lose its liberty, it will perish. Rome, Sparta and Carthage have perished. It will perish when the Legislature becomes more corrupt than the Executive." * When is that prophecy fulfilled in us? When may the Legislature be called "corrupt"? Not only when its members are bribed by Walpole with place or money. It is corrupt when it has destroyed its own balance by ceasing to consist of separate parts which check one another. It is corrupt when it so subordinates itself to the Executive that it loses control of legislation.† It must become corrupt when the electorate upon whom it depends ceases to care whether the constitution is unbalanced or not.

9

If, then, we try to re-think Montesquieu in terms of Western industrial democracy threatened by those whose method of conquest is always to destroy democracy from within, two fresh truths emerge from the *Esprit des lois*: first, that the

---

* *E.L.* xi. 6.

† On 5 February 1948, Mr. S. O. Davies (Merthyr, Lab.) in the House of Commons asked if the Prime Minister would cause an inquiry to be made into the circumstances responsible for the increasing amount of delegated legislation; the degree to which parliamentary responsibility had been handed over to unelected persons, and the consequent effects of this on the accepted rights and privileges of Members of Parliament and the people of this country. Mr. Attlee: No, sir. *The Times*, 6 February 1948.

people themselves, not being exempt from the rule that absolute power corrupts absolutely, must impose constitutional checks upon their own absolutism; and, secondly, that, in order to do this and be willing to do it, they must disengage the liberty of thought as a distinct and inalienable liberty. It may be necessary in time of war, and even in time of peace, to give to the Executive special powers to restrain the overt liberties; to grant these powers, if they are closely defined, is not necessarily to betray ourselves; but not to resist every attempt to mechanize the human mind is an ultimate betrayal.

Throughout Europe and in our midst these attempts are being continuously made. They take three principal forms: *first*, the teaching of economic fatalism; *second*, the perversion of the idea of equality *—the teaching that men are equal, not in the true sense of their being equal before God and before the law, but in the perverse sense of their being equal in their spiritual nothingness and in their subjection to their appetites; *third*, in the triple heresy of violence, chaos, and numbers— the teaching that, in the education of children or the policy of nations, the rule of value is the lust and anger of the mass; that law proceeding from a moral recognition of human dignity and difference is superstitious; that existence is to be regarded as a chaos of unrelated impulse; and, finally, that violence, as an expression of that impulse, is natural, necessary, and desirable. By these three main characteristics—of materialistic fatalism, of equality through appetite, and of violence exalted as a good in itself—the attack upon liberty at its source in the mind may be distinguished.

How may it be protected? It has first, I think, to be given, by the concerted action of the Western nations, security against armed attack and against those forms of enemy infiltration which operate against the mind but have not yet been given the legal status either of espionage or of seditious con-

* See also: " Maritain on Equality " in this book, page 195.

spiracy. It has next to be safeguarded, within each nation according to its conditions, by a great series of enactments to restore the Balance of the Constitution and the Liberties of the Subject. It has finally to be *enabled*, in every area of our social life, whether in departments of state or in trades unions or in schools, by positive laws to prevent not only the intimidation of minorities, but subversive intimidation *by* minorities. The difficulties are great and complex. It is not for me to legislate. I wish only to submit, and to submit urgently, that today attacks upon the mind have become as certainly overt acts as former attempts to imprison the body without trial. The shrinkage of the world, the development of the sciences of communication, the industrial clotting of populations, the penetration of men's homes, and the opportunities thus given to the use of fear as an instrument of psychological perversion called the War of Nerves, have exposed the liberty of thought to direct attack. As, in the past, Montesquieu related liberty to statesmanship, so are we now called upon to disengage the liberty of thought from the philosophic background of jurisprudence and make it cognizable by positive law. My prayer is that statesmen and jurists, whose experience far outreaches mine, may henceforth so regard it, and taking, in their courage and wisdom, measures to protect it, may, for the world's salvation, begin now to write a thirty-second book of the *Esprit des lois*.

THE ARTIST IN THE COMMUNITY *

AN analysis of the liberty of thought leads naturally to consideration of an artist's place in a free community: what is his duty towards it and what its duty towards him? I shall suggest, in the following pages, that the relationship between the artist and the community is, in one aspect, enduring, in that it arises from the nature of art and the nature of society itself; and, in another aspect, constantly changing, in that it arises from changes in artistic practice and in the forms which society assumes in different epochs. Finally, regarding this relationship between the artist and the community as in part constant, and in part variable, I shall inquire what the true relationship is now and is likely to become, and shall submit a concluding proposition: That by preserving this true relationship we may help to safeguard the liberty of thought and the community of freedom itself, for an artist is neither the community's priest nor the community's slave, but a member of it who holds in his especial charge certain qualities essential to its spiritual life. He is, as it were, the breath of the people's imagination without which they perish; and the people must learn, in each new phase of history, how to adjust themselves to art, how to receive it, how to make of it an ally with religion and science in every man's quest of truth; how, in each new climate, to breathe freely and deeply; for, if they do not, the authoritarians will stifle them, and the spirit of man, though it cannot die, be cast down, for long centuries, into obscurity and submission. Mrs. Charles Kingsley, in her Life of her husband, spoke a little strangely, as it may now seem to us, of

* The sixth W. P. Ker Memorial Lecture delivered in the University of Glasgow 18 April 1945.

her husband's "sympathy with Art, and deeper matters".
We may smile at her phrase but at the same time honour her
sense of art's relationship to all that she most valued in life.
We, in our turn, are called upon to re-gather our strength
from Athens and the Renaissance that, after the terrible
retrogression which our lives have witnessed, we may prepare
a way for what our children or our grandchildren, if they
survive, may dare to call the Re-enlightenment.

2

When, in the distant future, historians sit down to write,
what title will they give to the chapter which describes the
second half of the twentieth century? What is life going to
be about?

There are many who say that what lies before us is predominantly an economic struggle, and a few others—too few,
perhaps, for this is a subject which British public opinion
easily neglects—that our central problem will be of foreign
policy. Both views are reasonable, but they are evidently
interdependent, and there is danger in insisting on either of
them to the exclusion of the other. What is possible economically depends not upon abstract theory, Marxist or other, but
upon what our international relationships make possible; and
we forget at our peril that foreign policy is the condition and
sanction of home policy, and that security against foreign
enemies is a first charge on social security and economic
advance.

Among the principal subjects with which any historian of
our times will have to deal is our attempt to relate foreign
policy to economic policy and our ability to persuade ourselves, and to persuade others, to accept, for the sake of
gradually establishing an international law, certain limitations
upon national sovereignty. That this is the direction in
which peace-loving and unfanatical men will try to move the

world is scarcely open to doubt.   But will they be prevented by impatient and bloody extremists?   Our differences of economic theory and foreign policy cannot be resolved, can scarcely be profitably discussed, until we have answered within us the personal question: Do I speak and think as a free man or as an authoritarian?   Do I wish to live in a free community with men who differ from me in theory and faith, seeking with them—and with other nations—a reconciliation of practice, or am I determined to extirpate, in pursuit of what I believe to be right, whatever faith and theory differs from my own?

Some may feel that this presentation of the alternative is too abrupt.   British men and women of my own generation and of a generation older than mine may think so, for they were brought up in the habit of liberty as they were in the habit of peace.   They are as slow to believe in the possibility of totalitarianism in their own country as they were, in the first and third decades of the twentieth century, to believe that she would be involved in European war.   There are many in England and in America who regard all warnings as alarmist and all uncomfortable alternatives as too abrupt.   But the alternative will not be regarded as unreal in those European countries, from Spain and France to Poland and Greece, where the tyrannies and ideologies have stalked into men's homes; nor, I think, by Scotsmen and Englishmen of a generation younger than my own.   It is their life, not mine, that will carry the remaining burden of this century, and the Re-enlightenment, if they can win it, will be their children's, and perhaps their own, reward.

It was a very young man who first confronted me with this alternative.   He was a fighter-pilot, shot down and terribly burned in the Battle of Britain.   When he had recovered from his wounds, and the plastic surgeons had rebuilt his face, and he was struggling for that permission to fly again which,

being granted, led to his death, he came to dine at my house
in London.   Through all the bombardments, I had tried to
preserve one amenity there; we dined by candlelight and an
open fire; and I remember that, after dinner, we went upstairs, I with the decanter and he with the candelabra.   I
remember it because it was in the upstairs room, just after we
had entered it, that he, standing in mid-floor with a candelabrum
in each hand, said: " Nowadays, wherever I go, I ask myself
that question about everybody.   At dinner, I was asking it
about you."   For the moment I had lost his drift.   He was
carrying on our dinner-table conversation, and I meanwhile
had been thinking of other things.   " What question? " I
asked.   He put down the candelabra and told me, and we
talked of it half the night.

His point was this.   He felt that everyone in the modern
world—everyone, soldier, priest, scholar, tradesman or house-
maid—was potentially, whether he knew it or not, either a
Communist or a Nazi.   " Potentially," he insisted.   " As
yet, I'm neither myself.   But I know which way I'd go if I
had to choose.   And that's the question I ask myself about
other people: which way would they go if they had to choose?
Which way *will* they go *when* they have to choose?   Which
side are they on? "

I said: " Are they necessarily on either side? "

He answered: " Yes, I think they are, inside themselves.
I think they must be.   The world being what it is, a man
can't remain an indifferentist."

That was the word I challenged.   It seemed to me false to
suggest that the whole area of opinion lying between the two
opposed totalitarian polities was indifferent, neutral, colourless,
waiting only to drift helplessly into one or other of the warring
armies.

He said: " That at any rate is the impression that both
sides try to give.   To a great extent they are succeeding.

They are planting the idea that not to be in one camp or the other is a form of uncourageous compromise, and that the whole idea of freedom as a positive force is dead."

This was the discussion that held us into the night. He assumed that the battle to destroy the community of freedom was over or almost over, and that soon there would be no choice open except between one form of authoritarianism and another. Many in Europe feel as he did. The choice has been thrust upon them. I still believe that, in the long view of history, he and they will be seen to have been wrong. I think that it is in the destiny of the English-speaking peoples and, ultimately, after many vicissitudes, of a recovered France, to prove them wrong. But the other alternative remains. The question may not yet be: " To which Authoritarianism shall we submit?" Not yet: " To which slave-master shall we surrender ourselves?" But already and urgently the question is: " Shall we be bond or free?"

What the fighter-pilot said that night was a young man's evidence that the pressure of authoritarianism was heavy upon him. It is to be felt everywhere in the modern world, in the way in which religion is discussed, in the criticism of art on a basis of politics, in the penetration of common speech by ideological jargon, in the reluctance of so many men and women to defend their own opinion against the attack of extremists. It is to be felt, too, in the tendency, from which few of us are exempt, to be swayed by passing enthusiasms and passing indignations, to reverse our judgement of great issues and even of great nations in accordance with the swaying for-tunes of a battle or the flow of some popular emotion, to be carried forward by slogans and headlines rather than by the reasoned development and application of principle. There was alarming evidence of this tendency in our attitude towards the confusion which arose in Athens when the Germans had gone out. I happen to believe that our Government was right to intervene, but I will not now discuss the merits of that dispute.*   What was remarkable about it, and relevant to our present subject, was that, when the trouble began, a great part of British opinion, instead of suspending judgement and waiting to ascertain the facts, instead of trying to discover patiently where the true interest of freedom lay, aligned itself hastily on the Left or on the Right, and began to think and talk and write in terms of Party.   It was as if the minds of the British people had already begun to stiffen, to congeal into two clots of opinion, as if we had begun to lose our independence of judgement, our resilience of imagination, our power to refer each new problem, not to some rigid rule, but to our own consciences, our own sense of compassionate justice.   It is the radical principle and the invariable practice of all totalitarian systems to freeze imagination.   It is the radical principle of art to enable men and women to think and imagine for themselves.

If, therefore, the young airman's alternative is happily to be proved false; if the problem of the future is to have a non-totalitarian answer, it is important to understand what part an artist may play, and what part the community may enable him to play, in the solution of it.

3

What I am now seeking to discover is whether there are any elements in the nature of art and in the nature of society which may be said to establish an enduring undercurrent of relationship between them.   If these elements exist, if they are enduring like the tides, they will be a condition of the relationship between art and society in a particular epoch.

Now if anything in the doubtful history of our race is certain it is that before society existed there were men, and

* Though the temptation (1950) has not been decreased by the events of intervening years.

that before schools or coteries or classifications existed there was art. Indeed the first artist was presumably subjective. He made his work of art, his song or the picture he drew on the wall of his cave, in order to express his sense of happiness or fear, or *his* sense of the form of the natural object he depicted. In other words, his art sprang from within him; it was not at first designed to produce an effect upon others; but one day, as he was drawing on the wall to please no one but himself, his wife said: " My dear, that is not at all my idea of a mammoth. A mammoth, surely, has a longer tail ", and so the relationship of art to society was begun. All our æsthetic troubles, and perhaps all our matrimonial troubles, began in that moment, for the first artist, we may be sure, was both flattered and annoyed—flattered because he really had been drawing a mammoth and his wife had recognized it; annoyed because there was, after all, great variety in mammoths and wide scope for the interpretation of them in their relationship to rocks or mountains—it all depended on what *impression* they made upon you—and the first artist thought it unreasonable that his wife should concentrate on the length of the animal's tail. So he said: " It isn't a mammoth; it's what I feel about a mammoth "—half a lie, half a truth; and she said: " Well, anyhow, it isn't what I feel about a mammoth. Let us ask Belinda."

Belinda was their child, and when Belinda saw the picture she thought it was god; she fell down on her face and began to make propitiatory noises; and her father said: " Well, really, this is too much! " and the man within the artist slapped her soundly. But the artist within the man was flattered, and after a little while he began to say: " Well, after all, whether I intended it or not, the effect was that I drew Belinda's idea of god. Perhaps that is what art *is*."

Here, I think, he was right; he had, at any rate, hit upon one aspect of the truth; he had understood the relationship of his art to Belinda. There was, of course, another aspect of the truth, which no doubt troubled him again as soon as he took up another flint and began to scratch on another wall— namely, the relationship of his art to himself. Was he trying to reproduce a mammoth or, like Cézanne, to re-present it? Was he giving information about a mammoth, about the length of its tail for example, or was he, in his re-presentation of that debatable animal, giving information about himself? Or was he perhaps not giving information at all? Did he really care what his wife or what Belinda thought? There was a part of him, an extremely important part, that cared nothing for the effect of his drawing upon others or indeed for its likeness to a mammoth or a god; a part of him that was neither zoological nor theological nor social, nor even deliberately self-expressive; a part of him, an impulsive essence, the very seed of art, its innermost mystery, which, without rhyme or reason, said to him: " Draw! " so that he drew, not for his own sake or for society's sake or for god's sake or even for art's sake, but because something inside him said: " Draw! "

To this impulse, this absolute of art, many names are given. Some have spoken of it as " art for art's sake "; some as " art to the glory of God "; some as a desire for absolute beauty which, to them, is truth and " a joy for ever "; and in giving to the impulse these names they have unwittingly exposed it to the attack and ridicule of men who neither understand the names nor the thing. Let us beware how we attack or ridicule these names because perhaps to us one or other of them may seem limited or pretentious. Of course they are limited; they are an attempt to express the illimitable. Of course they sound pretentious; they are an attempt to express the inexpressible. Of course foolish cults grow up around them, clinging to the approximate name without having experienced the essential thing. But whatever the name, the impulse of art is holy and absolute as the impulse of love is holy and absolute, not to be traced to its origin, not to be accounted for by its effects, such an inward-feeling and out-ward-shining glory, such a " silence within the heart of a cry ", as you may see upon the face of Correggio's Io in the moment of her visitation by the god.   I wish to establish this ecstatic impulse, neither self-regarding nor world-regarding, as the essence of the artistic act—as it is the essence of the act of love—because, without its saving presence in our minds, we cannot hope to understand rightly the relationship of an artist to the community.   A hint of this relationship was given to the first artist when Belinda threw herself upon her face and began to worship not his mammoth but her own god.   To-wards his wife he had as an artist failed.   All she had said was that the animal's tail was too short.   Why had he failed? Because in her he had provoked nothing but a slavish desire to have reproduced for her what she had already seen; she wanted repetition and uniformity which, together, are hell, not imagination and variety which are a way to heaven; she was not provoked to a fresh imagining of anything—not even of a mammoth, much less of a god.   But with Belinda he had suc-ceeded because by his work of art she had been carried beyond his work of art; it had, so to speak, broken up the coagulation of her mind as a poker thrust into a sleepy fire breaks up the coagu-lation of the embers; and a flame had jumped out and burned and dazzled her, and her name for it was god.   It might not have been god.   It might have been anything—if she had been younger a divine doll, if a little older an almost divine lover. At all events, it was hers, not her father's: that is the point. It had grown in her soil, like a flower from a seed.   What her mother had wanted was what society so often demands of artists—something ready-made, useful and familiar, something that fulfilled her preconceptions and required of her neither adjustment nor growth nor imaginative effort of any kind, a clearly recognizable mammoth down to the last inch of its tail. But that was because the mind of Belinda's mother had become fixed, frozen, authoritarian, and the art of Belinda's father had failed to break it up. But with Belinda herself he had succeeded, and, when he had recovered from the shock of having his mammoth taken for a god, he said to himself: "I made the girl imagine for herself." And then he added: "That is what art is for. What art *is* is a different matter. I feel that inside myself, and Correggio will know and feel it when the time comes for him to paint Io in the moment of her visitation by the god. Meanwhile I know what art is for. It is to enable men to imagine for themselves." And he thought, in saying this, that he had solved the problem of the relationship of the artist to society, and I think he had taken a necessary step towards the solution of it; but he had not solved it because two vital questions remained unanswered and the answers to these differ, or appear to differ, from age to age.

4

These questions are: "By what means shall an artist enable men to imagine for themselves?" and, secondly: "What shall he enable them to imagine?" To the second question the authoritarian answer is simple: "The people shall not be enabled to imagine freely. They shall be compelled or persuaded or tempted to imagine what is good for them, and what is good for all is good for one and what is good for one is good for all." Sometimes the authoritarians dress up this answer in a more dignified and ancient dress, and say: "The people shall be made to imagine the Truth", and, when authority says that, we are on the way to the fire and the torture-chamber, to the death of Socrates, to the scourge and the crown of thorns. Why will men torment one another for the kingdom of this world, which is worthless when they have attained it? Why will they torment one another for the

kingdom of God, which is within them? If art has anything
to teach it is that these torments are vain, and that to mistake
one supposed aspect of truth for Truth itself and so to imprison men's curiosity and aspiration in the dungeon of an
ideology, is the unforgivable sin against the spirit of man.

An artist is bound by his vocation to recognize as sin the
authoritarian's claim to be a monopolist of truth. For that
very reason the word truth cannot be excluded from his
answers to the two vital questions. When he is asked what
he will enable men to imagine, he will answer, in summary:
" Aspects of Truth." When he is asked by what means he
will do this, he will answer, again in summary: " By communicating my own visions of Truth." You will observe
that the word " visions " is in the plural: " visions ", not
" vision "; you will remember that Thomas Hardy called a
volume of his poems *Moments of Vision*, and that he was
careful to renounce all claim to a monopoly of truth. " I
have no philosophy," he wrote, " merely what I have often
explained to be a confused heap of impressions, like those of a
bewildered child at a conjuring show." And you will not
have failed to notice that when that giant among artists,
Tolstoy, reached that stage of his life which is called his
" conversion "; when, that is to say, he exchanged his many
visions of truth for one vision of it and established an ethical
system; he became so much the less a practising artist and indeed repudiated art altogether as he had formerly understood
it. But Hardy's saying that he had no philosophy is not to be
understood to mean that he had no point of view. He stood
on a hill-top and from it surveyed experience, and it was his
own hill-top; he was not inconsistent in the sense of being
without distinct individuality; he was not for ever blown
hither and thither by the opinions of others, joining leagues
and clubs and fashionable groups and peering out at life
through their blinkers. He preserved his integrity, guarded

his individuality, looked out from his own hill-top. But he did not look only north, or only south, or only east or west. He did not fix upon a favourite view and say: " This is Truth. There is no other." He surveyed the whole landscape of experience with what eyes he had, and said to us: " Look: what do you see with your different eyes? " And we looked, and, though we did not see what he had seen, we saw what we had not seen before and might never have seen but for his visionary flash.

5

What is it then that an artist enables men to see? I think that ideally he enables them, looking out from the point of view of their own individualities, to see their own experience in a light of Truth—in *a* light, not *the* light, for there are many. But the phrase " in a light of Truth " is a vague one except to the man who uses it. I have used it, and cling to it, because it indicates to me something that is essential to my idea of the function of art in a community, but I will try to express in more concrete terms my answer to the question: " What is it that an artist enables men to imagine? "

An understanding of art's effect upon us, of its real value to mature men and women, may be reached by trying to remember what its effect was in childhood. Do you remember, can you still feel, what it was then to fall under the spell of a book? I remember well how, as I read, a circle seemed to be woven round me forbidding my thoughts to wander, so that attention became concentration, and concentration became at first effortless, then involuntary, then necessitous, and at last something more—absorption, self-surrender, a passing into another world. So the spell would fall. But the world into which I entered was never altogether the author's world, though I saw it by his light. My own identity was no more lost than a dreamer's identity is lost during his dream; but it was, as it were, distilled; what moved in the imagined world was not I, with the inhibitions of my self-consciousness, but the essence of I, freed from the knowledge that I was eight years old, or that I had a brother and two sisters, or that my preparation was not done, or that, if I walked round the little wood that bordered the tennis-lawn, I should come to the kitchen-garden: freed, that is to say, from the relationships of age, of person, of duty, of place, which tied me in my ordinary life: liberated from my social and temporal bonds, and yet liberated in such a way that I did not become, in the transition, anti-social, for I was liberated from my egotistical bonds as well.   This was the first part of the spell—liberation, intensi-fication, purification—a penetration of that film of personality to which name and circumstances are attached—a walking clean through the looking-glass.

On the other side of the looking-glass was not, as some pre-tend, an escape from life, but a new impulse and vitality.   On this side of the looking-glass we are bound by an unreal sense of order, of partition, of what is congruous and what incon-gruous; we think of time as if it were a calendar on the wall, each day to be stripped off in turn, the past, the present and the future impenetrable by one another; and this is spiritually untrue; all time is simultaneous; in my end is my beginning. On this side of the looking-glass, we are bound always by a sense that each individuality is locked within itself, so that, even between two people who love each other, though there is communication like the tapping on prison-walls, there is no fusion, and we struggle continually towards a fusion un-attainable in this world, giving many names to our struggle; sometimes the name of personal love, sometimes of friendship, sometimes of congregation in the worship of a god, sometimes of society or community.   Under the spell of art this separate-ness may be transcended.   On the other side of the looking-glass the prison walls are down.   There is inter-penetration of individuality, of time, of place. I well remember that, in childhood, under the spell of a story, I used to feel, without any sense of incongruity, that I myself was present at the Siege of Troy though I remained fully aware that the narrative belonged to the past; on my way home with Odysseus, I found Nausicaa playing ball with her maidens on a stretch of sea-shore where I had bathed yesterday; she had her own face, *and* the face of a beautiful girl whom I knew, *and* a face that was featureless, indescribable, like the face which Michelangelo left unpainted in his unfinished picture, " The Entombment"; she had many beauties, and, as well, an absolute beauty. And I knew, when I read of the Agony in the Garden, that where Jesus kneeled to pray was in a corner of the lawn in front of my own house, just as Giovanni Bellini knew, when he painted the scene, that Jesus kneeled on a little mound in the midst of an Italian landscape; and it seemed not unfitting or untrue that, within two hundred yards of this tennis lawn, was a steep dell or pit into which Joseph was cast by his brethren; nor was it unfitting or untrue.

And this breaking down by art of the compartments of the mind belongs not only to childhood. I first read Keats's *Eve of St. Agnes* when I was a young naval officer in the China Seas. My mind accepted the poet's description of his scene— the ancient castle, the bloodhound at the gate, the painted glass of the upper room.

> Full on this casement shone the wintry moon
> And threw warm gules on Madeline's fair breast,
> As down she knelt for heaven's grace and boon;
> Rose-bloom fell on her hands, together prest,
> And on her silver cross soft amethyst,
> And on her hair a glory, like a saint:
> She seem'd a splendid angel, newly drest
> Save wings, for heaven—

For me then, for me now, full on this casement shines the wintry moon, and yet, at the same time and with an enhancement, not a dissipation, of the illusion, it shines also into a cabin of H.M.S. *Monmouth* at sea, in which cabin for ever Madeline sleeps.

That is the spell of art which breaks down the divisions of time, place and circumstance, and sets the spirit free to go on its voyages. The greatest tribute that a writer earns from us is not that we keep our eyes fast upon his page, forgetting all else; but that sometimes, without knowing that we have ceased to read, we allow his book to rest, and look out over and beyond it with newly opened eyes, discovering all else. Then lies open to earthbound man the firmament of the spirit; he takes wing and travels in it, liberated from the chains of partial judgement and from the blindness of close appearances. Like a bird released from a cage, he soars, and sees truth in new aspects.

> Last night I flew into the tree of death;
> Sudden an outer wind did me sustain;
> And I, from feathered poppet on its swing,
> Wrapt in my element, was bird again.*

And though the spell of art breaks at last and he returns to earth, it is not to the cage of his former prejudice that he returns. The spell of art breaks, the *Eve of St. Agnes* is ended; the young officer finds himself in the cabin again, feels the throb of engines, listens to the whirr of an electric fan. It is five minutes to eight bells, and he goes on to the bridge to keep his middle-watch. But he has been a liberated spirit, and thereafter, in all life's embittered divisions, in all his faults and follies and self-imprisonments and hardnesses of heart, he never altogether ceases to be aware of the unity of the living with the dead, and in all his temptations to hatred or fear he cannot be without compassion. Art has planted in him a seed from which his own imagination shall spring; has fertilized

* *Sparkenbroke*, II, 5.

his earth that of it he may be reborn.   An artist does not
renew society; he enables men to renew themselves and so, in
the long run, the society in which they live.

6

In saying this, in suggesting what an artist may enable men
to imagine, I have, perhaps, already implied an answer to the
other vital question: how does an artist produce this effect?
I shall not here elaborate that answer, for I do not wish to
plunge into a discussion of technical processes or into a
matching of one school with another.   I seek a common
factor, and this much, I think, is clear: that if the true effect of
art is to enable men to re-value their own experience in terms
of the absolute values—that is to say, in terms of Compassion,
Beauty and Truth—the artist himself must value life in those
terms and must be able to communicate his valuation in a way
that is not merely a statement of his opinion or even an account
of his vision but is fertilizing.

This view of the function of art receives endorsement as
soon as we ask ourselves what the difference is between a good
book, important in its own age, and an immortal book which
has continuing life in generation after generation.   When you
and I read the Decameron of Boccaccio or the Sonnets of
Shakespeare or Emily Brontë's *Wuthering Heights,* our pleasure
and excitement are not the same as the pleasure and
excitement in which these masterpieces were written.   We
are different creatures, nurtured in a different age, and what
we imagine is not what those dead writers imagined.   In
brief, their books are alive because their life is renewed in us,
because we re-imagine them; and their genius consists in
their power to enable us to do so, in their fertilizing power.
They are not beautiful flowers pressed in an album; they
seed, and, though they die in one generation of men, they bring
forth in another.   So Keats, who was far removed from

Boccaccio and did not see what he saw, was nevertheless inspired by a story of Boccaccio's to write *Isabella or the Pot of Basil*, and we, reading *Isabella*, though we do not see what Keats saw, are impregnated by his vision to bring forth our own.

Now if we agree that, from the point of view of the community, what is important in an artist is his impregnating-power, and that, from the point of view of an artist, what is important in the community is its power to be impregnated and to re-present his vision in an eternal vitality and freshness, does it not follow in the first place that the subject of a work of art, though important, has not, and cannot have, the primary importance that a part of modern criticism, and particularly authoritarian criticism, is inclined to attach to it?

The subject of a story or a poem (and I continue to speak in terms of literature, though the same principle may be applied to the other arts) the subject of a story or a poem is evidently important because neither story nor poem can exist without a subject; but the subject is not the essence or the immortal, fertilizing quality of the work of art, but a limitation upon it. No one, unless he is a historian in quest of material, now reads Dickens because he wrote about prison-reform or Turgenev because he wrote about liberalism in Russia or Victor Hugo because he attacked Napoleon the Third; and no one in the future will read Wells because he once chose as his subject certain doctrines of the Fabian Society. Or, rather, people may *read* these authors because they are interested now or in the future in subjects related to these subjects, but their own imaginations will not be fertilized by the subject—for then any pamphlet would serve as well—but by the excitement with which the author wrote about the subject. The fertilizing power is not the subject, but the æsthetic passion which the author pours into it; and this æsthetic passion is expressed not in subject alone or in treatment alone but in a harmony between

them.   Therefore we are not to say, except at the peril of an
ultimate sterility: " This subject is admissible, that subject is
barred," or: " This treatment is admirable, that treatment is
ruled out," and this is precisely what the authoritarians of all
ages do say.   It is madness and folly for us to cry: " But we
are modern.   Our particular brand of authoritarianism really
is right.   Our preference for free verse—or what you will—
really is the last word in prosody.   Our particular swerve
towards ecclesiasticism or proletarianism or romanticism or
realism—or what you will—really is the law and the prophets."
In saying this, we are ourselves committing all the sins which
we condemn in others as we read the history of literature.   We
say of Victorian criticism that it insisted too much on the
religious or ethical content of the work it criticized.   And so
it did.   But it knew what it was doing; according to its lights
it could sometimes be wonderfully fair, and we find that when
Mrs. Humphry Ward published *Robert Elsmere*, a novel which
struck to the very heart of Victorian religious controversy,
The Spectator could say:

> Profoundly as we differ from Mrs. Humphry Ward's criticism
> of Christianity we recognize in her book one of the most striking
> pictures of a sincere religious ideal that has ever yet been presented
> to our generation under the disguise of a modern novel.

How many modern reviews are there which, being wedded to
one or other of the authoritarian ideologies or even to one of
our slightly less ferocious economic " isms ", would thus praise
on its merits the work of a writer from whom they " profoundly
differed "?   In the period between the war of 1914 and the
war of 1939, a powerful section of criticism looked upon certain
subjects and certain treatments with such horror that they
were excluded from discussion and from the anthologies.
With the exception of one unrepresentative poem about
clouds, Rupert Brooke was completely shut out from Yeats's
Oxford Book of Modern Verse; his war poems and his love

poems were treated as if they were obscene. In the same volume another poet of the same generation, Robert Nichols, is given a place, but his war poems also are unrepresented. Yeats would not give room to this, which will live when two-thirds of the poems he included are forgotten:

> Was there love once? I have forgotten her.
>   Was there grief once? Grief yet is mine.
> O loved, living, dying, heroic soldier,
>   All, all, my joy, my grief, my love are thine!

And if Yeats, a great poet, compiling not a personal anthology but an Oxford book, could be thus cabined by a partisan distaste for certain subjects and treatments, how much fiercer and narrower was the partisanship of the camp-followers whose very livelihood depended upon their closely following the camp! They took the view that art should, in its subject, reflect what Yeats call their " social passion " and what I should call their political fanaticism. They insisted further that certain treatments, certain ways of writing, should be regarded as the brand of Cain. They howled against romanticism as Victorian spinsters howled against sex.

> Great Heaven! When these with clamour shrill
>   Drift out to Lethe's harbour bar
> A verse of Lovelace shall be still
>   As vivid as a pulsing star.

The verse is William Watson's, and Yeats himself quoted it in his preface to the Oxford Book. How strange that he should quote it and himself fall into the very error that it condemned!

No: we are not to dictate to an artist either subject or treatment, nor are we to deny to him any subject or any treatment. We are not schoolmistresses. We are not censors. All that matters is that the subject be one that awakes the artist's æsthetic passion, and that the harmony between subject and treatment be such that it casts a spell upon him, enabling him to be visited by his god, and so casts a spell upon us, enabling us to be visited by ours. " The excellence of every art ", said Keats, " is——" What a wonderful beginning of a sentence! If the page of Keats's manuscript had ended there and the next page been lost, the world would have been breathless to know how the sentence continued. " The excellence of every art ", said Keats, " is——" and he did not say that it was in its subject or in its treatment, still less that it was in its social passion or its adherence to any ethical system or in its contemporaneousness. " The excellence of every art ", said Keats, " is its intensity." And what did he mean by that? Fortunately he tells us. " Capable ", he continues, " of making all disagreeables evaporate from their being in close relationship with Beauty and Truth." Do not misunderstand him. By " disagreeables " he does not mean things that are unpleasant to us; he means those things which do not agree together, which clash in our immediate experience, but which harmonize when seen in the aspect of eternity. Keats's " disagreeables " are what I have called our incongruities, of time, of place, of individuality, of right seemingly opposed to right, of loyalty conflicting with loyalty. It is the function of art by its intensity to penetrate these incongruities, to perceive some aspect of order in the chaos of living, some aspect of beauty in that order, some aspect of truth in that beauty, and so to distil experience that we are made partakers of its essence and are enabled to re-imagine it and to renew ourselves.

7

It would seem then that though, as I suggested at the outset, art continually changes its practice and society its forms so that to us, who float upon the surface of experience, there appears to be a variable relationship between them, and though, in a sense, the relationship *is* variable and we have continually to adjust ourselves to it, the adjustments we make should always be so designed as to preserve the true and essential relationship.   This willingness to see the artist as an impregnator of the spirit of man and not as a propagator of his own, or our own, opinions, is of the more importance in a period of swift and radical social change.   The tendency of our time is for human thought, alarmed by the rapidity of change, by the seeming dissolution of society into a condition of flux, to congeal into stiff, uniform chunks of fierce and frightened orthodoxy—the orthodoxy which condemned Keats because he did not write like Pope, the orthodoxy which condemned Swinburne because he was unchristian, the orthodoxy which in our own day invented the ignorant word "escapist" and pretends that social consciousness is the criterion of art.   And so we are in danger of demanding, as authoritarians do, that an artist fall in with our platoon, or of insisting that he must be in our sense a good citizen before we will regard him as a good artist.   In fact it is probably desirable that an artist should be, as a man, a good citizen; that he should obey the laws and fight his country's enemies and care for the happiness of the people.   It is probably desirable that he should do these things because, if he does them, the experience may be valuable to him, and, if he does not, he may fall into opposition to the State and waste his energies either in exile or in struggles important to him as a man but irrelevant to him as an artist.   But though good citizenship may be desirable in him, it is evidently not always so; certainly we are not qualified to define good citizenship for him and to reject him, as an artist, because as a man he does not conform to our definition.   Do we condemn Thomas Mann because by Nazi standards he has not been a good citizen of his own German state?   Do we exclude Shelley because, as a citizen, his behaviour was extremely odd?   No: we may enforce our laws upon the man but not our opinions upon the artist.   And he, in his turn, must understand that, though he is entitled to express his opinions, he is no more entitled to drill the community than the community is entitled to drill the artist in him. He is entitled to express his opinions if the subject of those opinions is what at the moment stirs his æsthetic passion; in this way, great religious poetry has been produced; but woe to him if his art does not transcend his didacticism and carry him away from it and beyond it! Woe even to Shelley if he had not so often and so gloriously forgotten to be a propagandist! Immortality is not to be voted at a political meeting. Posterity will not stay in any man's school. We are wilful and enchanted children, by the grace of God. Our school-classes and our school-books and our school-rewards and punishments matter very little to us in the end. For an hour or two we may earnestly concern ourselves with them, and turn our solemn, communal eyes on the teacher who presides over these things; but what in our heart of hearts we want to know about is the world beyond this classroom of his. He whom we love and remember is not he who thrusts upon us his own dusty chart of the Supreme Reality, scored over with his arguments, prejudices and opinions; nor he who will draw a map of heaven on the blackboard and chastise us with scorpions if we will not fall down and worship it; but he who will pull the curtain away from the classroom window and let us see our own heaven with our own eyes. And this enablement of mankind, I take to be the function of true education, for the very word means a leading-out, and to lead out the spirit of man, through the wise, liberating self-discipline of learning and wonder, has been the glory of great teachers and of great Universities since civilization began to flower.

We are citizens, but we are men and women; we are men and women, but we are spirits. We live in the spirit, though we are instructed in the mind—

> The mind, that ocean where each kind
> Does straight its own resemblance find;
> Yet it creates, transcending these,
> Far other worlds and other seas.

And to these, and to the truth that dwells in them, we come
not by instruction but by vision, the vision that penetrates to
the spirit through the senses. Shelley knew; he stopped
preaching and drew attention to something that was not a
bird and far transcended the skylark. Keats knew: he did
not preach at all, and in his vision forgot even the nightingale.
And Hardy knew:

> Love is, yea, a great thing,
>   A great thing to me,
> When, having drawn across the lawn
>   In darkness silently,
> A figure flits like one a-wing
>   Out from the nearest tree:
> O love is, yes, a great thing
>   A great thing to me!
>
> Will these be always great things,
>   Great things to me? . . .
> Let it befall that One will call,
>   " Soul, I have need of thee ":
> What then? Joy-haunts, impassioned flings,
>   Love, and its ecstasy,
> Will always have been great things,
>   Great things to me!

So let us not think too communally on the relationship of the
artist and the community, for along that path of thought lie
the gauleiters on the one hand and the commissars on the
other. What then? As you like it or what you will.

>   . . : Joy-haunts, impassioned flings,
>   Love, and its ecstasy . . .

skylarks, nightingales! Take them, but take them into yourselves. Give the artist freedom that he may discover; preserve yourselves in freedom that you may receive and re-create.

Go out and find him.   You will recognize a true artist easily
enough nowadays, for he will not be wearing a party-badge:

> 'Tis the man who with a bird,
> Wren, or Eagle, finds his way to
> All its instincts; he hath heard
> The Lion's roaring, and can tell
> What his horny throat expresseth
> And to him the Tiger's yell
> Comes articulate and presseth
> On his ear like mother-tongue.

That is the artist.   You are the community.   Lions and skylarks, tigers and nightingales, eagles and wrens, love and its
ecstasy—all are subjects of art and all are at your disposal.
But do not conscribe them.   Do not bring them into the class-
room and stuff them and stick labels on them—for, to do that,
you must kill them first.

III. INSTANCES

THE DARK AGES or *The Liberty Not to Despair*

IMAGINING THE FUTURE or *The Liberty to Build*

MASTER AND PUPIL or *The Liberty of Teaching*

OLD KASPAR'S WORK UNDONE or *The Liberty to Have Roots*

THE GLOW OF LIVING or *Liberty in Time*

THE WINE AND THE BOTTLE or *The Liberty to Enjoy and Accept*

THE DARK AGES
OR
THE LIBERTY NOT TO DESPAIR

A MEDIEVALIST treads guarded territory which the rest of us have not the means to explore. Later centuries will yield their secrets to our study, but what we learn of the Middle Age must be learned at second-hand, for High German and a dozen other tongues are needed if we are to hear the period speak. So poor is our own equipment that we are, to a great extent, incapable even of receiving what scholars of this subject have to give us in our own language, for their text is pointed by quotations which require a knowledge that we have not. Nevertheless, as we peer out from the darkness of our own world and ask ourselves whether indeed civilization is all over bar the mourning, as we seek for the queer reassurance that there have been passages of history worse than ours which mankind has survived, we are strongly drawn to those centuries which have been called the Dark Ages. Dark? we say hopefully. Darker than this? If that were true, it would be at any rate an encouragement to dream of another Renaissance. So we take up again the books that H. W. C. Davis taught us to read at Oxford long ago. To study them, to sit at the feet of W. P. Ker for a week or two, to plunge once more into Helen Waddell's masterpiece, *The Wandering Scholars*, and be led by her parallel translations to the verses of Alcuin or Boethius or Abelard is to rediscover at least enough of the mystery to be made humble. We tread ignorantly; but the learnèd doctors would not forbid us to ask questions or to seek, in those Dark Ages, if we may find it amid their starry wonders, a consolation for our own.

There is none, it would seem, on the grounds that they were darker, unless light be understood to mean knowledge reckoned quantitatively—a reckoning for barbarians. Even if we do not take into consideration the whole Middle Age between Claudian and the Revival of Learning but choose for more flattering comparison with ourselves the Dark Ages proper—that is to say, the period before 1100—there is rich evidence that the men of those days, at any rate those who wrote books, were less despairing than their modern counterparts. To Victorian self-confidence not the Dark Ages only but the whole Middle Age appeared benighted. Ker quotes Cotter Morison as having described the thousand years between the fifth and the fifteenth centuries as

a hollow in which many great, beautiful and heroic things were done and created, but in which knowledge, as we understand it, and as Aristotle understood it, had no place. The revival of learning and the Renaissance are memorable as the first sturdy breasting by humanity of the hither slope of the great hollow which lies between us and the ancient world. The modern man, reformed and regenerated by knowledge, looks across it and recognizes—

recognizes, in brief, the kinship of his own enlightenment with the civilizations of Athens and Rome. Who shall sneer at that passage as complacent? Cotter Morison was a scholar and no fool. Writing in 1887, he was expressing the intelligent confidence of his time. But the words are astonishing to us. If the Dark Ages and, indeed, the " middle " centuries that produced Chartres and Dante were a " hollow ", who shall measure our pit?

An excerpt from Sacheverell Sitwell's *Splendours and Miseries* may be read beside Cotter Morison.

Was not the world old and evil in the past? Yes! But it was infinite. No one knew its ends. The horror of this is that it is finite.

And speaking of the lost chances of saving the world, Mr. Sitwell adds :—

But there is no hope of that in our life-time, and we are driven in upon ourselves. Two wars have destroyed the opportunities. The new-born babe lies in the shadow of the third war, that is to come, and that will be more horrible than all the others.

Thus far has the point of view of art and scholarship moved in sixty years. Then, modern man was able to feel that, as an inheritor of the Renaissance, he stood, " reformed and regenerated by knowledge ", on civilization's upward slope; now, for him, the finiteness of his world is the horror of it, his extended knowledge is the reaching out of his hands to touch everywhere a prison wall, and when he looks out from the place where he stands it is not to recognize his kinship with the Athenian splendour but rather to see in " the hollow " glories lost, and upon " the hither slope " a missing of chances now irretrievable.

Are we to say, then, either that Cotter Morison was grossly self-deceived or that Sacheverell Sitwell is without reason? If not, if each is a pointer to the truth of his own age, how, in so short a time, has the world been so disastrously perverted? The answer must be that the seed of disaster lay already in the Victorian aspiration and that the climate of our folly or wickedness has brought it to monstrous fruit. The tendency of all our shallower thinking is to blame the wars, and to find scapegoats. But wars are an effect; the cause is not in them or even in those men whose ambition fires the charge, but in ourselves; just as our happiness or despair depends upon what we find when " we are driven in upon ourselves ". Was not the world old and evil in the past? There were wars then. " *O tristia sæcula priora*," wrote the timid and unwarlike

Eugenius Vulgarius more than a thousand years ago.   Helen
Waddell translates him:—

> O sorrowful and ancient days
>   Where learned ye to make sepulchres?
> Who taught you all the evil ways
>   Wherein to wound men's souls in wars?

But nowhere in those distant centuries, though there are com-
plaints and sadness and often bitter outcry against life's cruelty,
is there the grinding harshness of modern despairs.   If we
ask why, the readiest answer—and a just answer—is that the
voices which come to us from " the hollow " were, in many
instances, Christian, or of men who, even in a dungeon under
torture or the threat of torture, had, like Boethius, the consola-
tions of philosophy, and could say of the heavens:

> So Love still guides their deathless ways,
> And ugly Hate that maketh wars
> Is exiled from the shore of stars.

But this is not the whole answer or, more accurately, it is not
that part of the answer which applies most closely to us.   If
what we are looking for is the seed, present in the nineteenth
century, which has borne so ugly a fruit in our own times, and
if we would discover an indication of the nature of that seed
in a contrast between ourselves and the Dark Ages, it is not
enough to speak in general terms of their Christianity or of
their philosophy.   We must particularize.   They too suffered.   They too lived in an age in which barbarians had
quenched, or nearly quenched, the light of civilization.   What
is the special poison in us which has made our poets desperate
with a despair that is so evidently different in kind from the
medieval?

First to be named is, perhaps, our increasing awareness that
we have not been, and are not being, " reformed and regenerated by knowledge ", but that, on the contrary, the accumula-

tion and swelling of unrelated knowledge has broken the moral order of our universe. This subject leads now, in the context of the Dark Ages, to another—to a comparison between their approach to the idea of common humanity and our own, for upon the meaning that men attach to this phrase and upon the nature of their loyalty to it their concept of a moral order greatly depends. Neither suffering nor even terror produces despair in men; loneliness and boredom are the prime cause of it, and they are the miseries that beset our crowded and eventful age.

The remedy for them is a sense of our common humanity and an undying outgoing interest in it. This we ourselves and our forward-looking predecessors of the nineteenth century have always professed. The words " common humanity " have been continually on Europe's lips since new thoughts began to stir in her mind in the latter half of the eighteenth century. Again and again—in the United States, in revolutionary France, in the upheavals and idealisms of '48, in the emancipation of slaves, the development of social legislation at home, the creation of a new Russia and the vain struggle at Geneva and, most recently, in the United Nations—attempts have been made to translate the idea of common humanity into political terms. When Cotter Morison wrote, men believed that, in spite of every disappointment and set-back, they were succeeding and would succeed, and they believed too that this was what life chiefly required of them. Though, in a great part of Victorian England, the political aspect of the idea of common humanity was still seen in the light of a moral order, and the emphasis of Maurice's Christian Socialism still lay upon the adjective, the influence of the French Revolution was great—great enough to lead humanitarians to think more and more that what men have in common, the element to be fostered and cultivated, is their membership of a political community. The political community chosen for exaltation varied.   To some it was an empire, to some a class, to some the parliament of man.   Different though these doctrines were and preached by men of seemingly opposed idealisms, they were all directed towards a political interpretation of the idea of common humanity.

For a time, all seemed to be well, and, in a sense, was well. The idea does require political interpretation, and neither the Victorians nor ourselves have been wrong to accept from the French Revolution this part of its teaching.   But to allow a political interpretation of the idea to eat up all other interpretations of it; to insist—as many Victorians did and as we have done and are still doing—that a man's link with other men is mainly political is to lay him open to despair whenever, in war or peace, political organization breaks down.   Then, for him, political disorder is chaos indeed.   If membership of a nation or of a class or of a party is the whole meaning of common humanity; if, even, membership of a world-community of political animals is taken to be its whole meaning; then, inevitably, when war after war strikes him and organized society is in rout, a man is without resources, his whole faith is broken.   Exiled from common humanity as he has been taught to understand it, he is lonely, bored and desperate.

The men of the Dark Ages were exempt from our despair, though not from our sorrows, and the reason seems to be that their notion of common humanity was altogether different from ours.   Of a part of this difference we are entitled to be proud.   Though the dwellers in " the hollow " were not ignorant of communal life and great beauty sprang from their ordering of it; though, even outside the monasteries, the feudal system was very far from being that mingling of irresponsible privilege with serfdom that bad teachers of democracy pretend that it was; and though the men of the Middle Age had much to tell of internationalism itself which we should do well to learn, it is open to us to claim, if we will, that in a thousand years political understanding, if not yet political application, of the idea of common humanity has made some advance. The Statute of Westminster and the Constitution of the United States are more mature political documents than the tenth century could have produced. Let us, for our credit's sake, count it as gain, and yet recognize that the men of " the hollow " held something which we have lost and might yet recover—a view of their link with other men that saved them from our loneliness of disintegration. However their society was attacked by war, pestilence and famine, however near it came or seemed to come to disintegration, this link was unbroken. For them, what men had in common was not their membership of any community, unless it was a spiritual one, but their possession of five senses and a soul. Their membership of certain communities, religious or secular, was extremely important in their eyes, but it was, for them, the branch, not the root; the root was in the soul and, through the soul, in God, or, if the community were secular—for example, if it were an order of chivalry—the root was in the personality and, through the personality, in the chivalric idea, itself in part religious.

Thus, because their intuition of common humanity had not its root in what was destructible in society but in what is inalienable from man—his senses and his soul, this intuition did not forsake them, however great the worldly disaster they suffered. This seems to have been true of men who were neither virtuous nor devout. The violent, the cruel, the sensual, the ambitious, whose treasure was by no means in heaven, however they might rage against loss when they suffered it, did not by reason of that loss despair of life itself. The loss was personal and accidental; they blamed it on their luck, on their enemies or on themselves. Neither they nor the men of religion felt, as modern men thinking in terms of the community are apt to feel, that their afflictions were evidence of a failure of the human purpose. Sometimes, no doubt, they went out and hanged themselves, but they did not put the neck of all mankind into the noose of their communal despair.

No one, in brief, who reads a little of what was written in those days, whether the writing be sacred or profane, can miss the conclusion that, in comparison with these men, we, by emphasizing continually the political aspect of our humanity, have become dehumanized; that the seed of this bleak heresy was present in the Victorians and that the fruit of it is our despair. There is something altogether modern about it— modern, that is to say, in the sense in which everything that has followed the last decades of the eighteenth century may be called modern. Before that, before the idea of common humanity received a political bias from which it has never recovered, it is hard to find in all history any counterpart of the special, dehumanized barrenness of our laments. Over two thousand years ago (the learned translator E. R. Hughes gives the date as the middle of the fourth century B.C.) the Chinese author of *The Great Learning* wrote:—

It is said in the *Book of Ch'u*: "The State of Ch'u has nothing it considers precious except its good men. Them it holds precious. Uncle Fan said: ' As exiles there is nothing we count precious, only to be human-hearted to our kin.' "

And in *The Mean-in-Action* is this:—

It is only the man who is entirely real in this world of experience who has the power to give full development to his own nature. . . .

There is a wonderful echo in that hymn of Prudentius for the burial of the dead which begins *Nunc suscipe, terra, fovendum*, and ends:—

nec si vaga flamina et auræ
    vacuum per inane volantes
tulerint cum pulvere nervos
    hominem periisse licebit.
(Not though wandering winds and idle
    Drifting through the empty sky,
Scatter dust was nerve and sinew
    Is it given man to die.)

Prudentius flourished in the second half of the fourth century, a contemporary of Augustine and Ambrose. " He does not speak ", says Miss Waddell, " of any formal vows . . . yet his phrases are the naked poetry of religion," and this " naked poetry " runs down through the ages.   A falling away from it, and not a refusal of " formal vows ", is what seems to distinguish the unhappiness of our age from the unhappinesses that have preceded it.

IMAGINING THE FUTURE
OR
THE LIBERTY TO BUILD

WHAT lies ahead in the imagining of men and girls now in their twenties? What do they themselves desire? What kind of life do they propose, if they can have it? What are they willing to pay? It is useless to say that there is no answer to these questions. We may be unable to discern the answer, but it exists nevertheless. Social historians, looking back upon our times, will observe their divergence from the Victorian and post-Victorian ages and will say: This or this was the drift of opinion, this or this was the kind of life that Englishmen in the middle of the twentieth century began to strive for; and, if they are human historians with an eye for something else than economic statistics, they will seek their evidence everywhere—in the pleasures of the people, in their imaginative literature and even in their day-dreams.

A girl of this age lately spoke to her father these illuminating words: "You spent your time, when you were young, in breaking down the walls. We are going to build them up again." Her remark was found, upon investigation, to have sprung from three things: her own experience of a scattered, harassed, over-worked and regimented life, her interpretation of Trollope and her reading of Trevelyan's *English Social History*. The concluding chapters of Trevelyan, on Victorian England, had filled her with what can only be described as a firmly reasonable nostalgia. Did she wish to return to Victorianism? She rightly dismissed the question. Of what use to discuss the impossible? In any case, there was evidently a Victorian " stuffiness " and, in her mind, a Victorian injustice and hypocrisy to which she had no wish to return. Nevertheless, there were in that age certain things—human things, not Victorian things exclusively—that she hankered after. People had time to think. You could be interested in subjects that were not immediate matters of life and death. Every hope was not governed by a threat. Every discussion did not end in a bomb. " Even politics ", she said, " was an argument, not a scramble for crumbs."

Like many of her generation, she had been discovering Trollope, for it is altogether false to suppose that the revival of Trollope is a consequence of the desire of such Victorians as survive to lose themselves in the past. He is read with devotion by the young, who beg or borrow him, and, during the recent war, passed him from hand to hand almost conspiratorially, as if Mrs. Proudie and Lily Dale were members of an underground movement and all the Barsetshire novels were published in an Edition de Minuit. What had struck this girl as odd, interesting and, in a sense, enviable, was Trollope's account, in his Autobiography, of his political theory— enviable, not because she agreed with his theory, but because he was able to express it in the way he did. Confronted by " the terrible inequalities that we see ", he confessed himself unable to " understand the operations of Almighty wisdom " in this matter, but made it clear that he had no intention of interfering with them.

This consciousness of wrong has induced in many enthusiastic but unbalanced minds a desire to set all things right by a proclaimed equality. In their efforts such men have shown how powerless they are in opposing the ordinances of the Creator. For the mind of the thinker and the student is driven to admit, though it be awestruck by apparent injustice, that this inequality is the work of God.

The young thinker of our own times was by no means driven

to admit this, but she was aware of Trollope's sincerity and fascinated by his ensuing argument.

Trollope's point was that he could not share the opinion either of an urgent equalitarian who presented " to the imaginations of men ideas of communism, of ruin, and insane democracy ", or of a " conscientious, philanthropic Conservative " who, " being surely convinced that such inequalities were of divine origin, told himself that it was his duty to preserve them ". Trollope steered a middle course in his approach to the Almighty wisdom. Not only was " the divine inequality " apparent to him, but—and this was what Conservatives missed—" the equally divine diminution of that inequality ". He regarded this continual diminution as a series of steps towards the human millennium, " a tendency towards equality ", and he was, as a genuinely advanced Conservative-Liberal, " even willing to help the many to ascend the ladder a little ", though he was aware that this would mean his coming down to meet them.

It is a remarkable passage in a remarkable book. We may think that Trollope's reluctance to expedite the operations of the Almighty wisdom was unduly cautious. But it was not this that principally interested his young admirer. What astonished and pleased her was his " complacency ". And why did it please her? " Well," she said, " because he had at any rate made up his own mind. You can agree or disagree with his moral principle, but he had one." She pointed to another passage which she had marked :—

The truth of all this I had long taken home to myself. I had now been thinking of it for thirty years, and had never doubted. But I had always been aware of a certain visionary weakness in myself in regard to politics.

" Visionary ! " she exclaimed. " What a world, in which Trollope was a visionary ! But what a world in which anyone could think of anything for thirty years and never doubt it!

The Victorians had walls.   Your generation broke them down.
It's draughty without them."

If by " walls " we mean the common acceptance of certain
rules which restricted and protected areas of life as a wall
restricts and protects a garden, then it is true that the poor
as well as the rich were enclosed by them in Trollope's day.
Above the level of abject poverty there were few, of whatever
class, who did not feel themselves to be at once restricted and
protected by habits, customs, relationships, and principles
which seemed to them enduring.   Life was at once firmly
rooted and expanding.

This, with the idea of ordered progress implied in it, was
made possible by the sense, which all men had then, that time
was continuous.   Trollope was not impatient of the admittedly slow operation of the Almighty wisdom because he
believed in his heart that there was time enough.   Unless
some extraordinary accident befell, the young man of promise
who today was apprenticed to a trade or went to Oxford or
married a wife would not tomorrow be snatched away from
his trade, his education or his family, and in a month, perhaps,
be dead.   Nor was it at all likely that anything worse than an
occasional outburst of jingoism would perturb the smooth
surface or divert the even flow of English political thought.
Once the French Revolution was well behind, the Reform
Bill passed and the Forties discreetly navigated, there might
be storms and hot disagreements among the crew, but there
was no general fear of shipwreck.   So in literature: you were
an official of the Post Office, you hunted three times a week,
you played whist pretty regularly at the Garrick Club, you
stood for Parliament, you dined out in the Season, and yet, by
rising at 5.30 each morning, you poured out a stream of novels
good enough to be clamoured for by young and old eighty
years later.   You did all these things, if you were Trollope,

because it was then reasonably possible to plan your day, your month, your year, even your life; and you were able to make these plans, to be sure of them, because you were sure of yourself; and you were able to be sure of yourself because your garden had walls.

For the same reason, if your spirit was bolder than Trollope's, if you were Darwin, for instance, or Matthew Arnold or Florence Nightingale, you were able to make formidable sorties which were of great interest to your opponents as well as to your friends. These advances often caused society to readjust its ramparts, to amend its rules, but they did not disintegrate society. Far from being " stuffier ", the Victorian age was in many respects much more intellectually courageous, independent and experimental than our own, partly, it is true, because its energies were not perpetually drained away, but chiefly because it had less reason to be afraid. You can go exploring, if your home will not vanish in your absence. You can experiment in a society where there is a margin of error. But he is a rash man who goes out tilting at windmills when bandits are about, and a bold one who, in order that he may read the book of wisdom, lights a match in a powder-magazine.

If the young of our own time seem now and then strangely unadventurous and unenterprising, it should be borne in mind not only that adventure by them has been deprived of its reward, but that they have long to live in this unpromising world. They are exceedingly well aware that the walls of their home are down and that there are bandits about. In the circumstances, it is not surprising that a girl should read Trevelyan's final chapters with a " firmly reasonable nostalgia ", though it does not appear to be in the least true that a " reaction " has set in and that Victorianism is being uncritically romanticized. Even this is not impossible. If there should be a spate of Victorian plays; if Victorian dresses, or dresses very like them, should return; if every one should begin again to call on every one else and even scandal become solemn, the oddity would be pardonable by all except those who will not allow the chariot of Progress to pause even to water its horses or tie a new ribbon on its whip.   But a romantic revival of Victorianism seems not to be in the air or to be at any rate but a very small part of what is in the air.   When the girl said to her father that she and her generation intended to build up the walls again, she was speaking inaccurately, as is the habit of her kind.   She did not mean that she would build the same walls but others of her own architecture.

The first wall necessary is that upon which all that was good in Victorianism depended—the wall of European peace. Power always was, and will always be, the foundation of it. It cannot be built of paper however many signatures are written on it.   If the West should again fail to maintain it in sufficient power, no other wall that the young build, certainly no other " social service ", can be of value. Nothing else will make possible those experiments within a margin of safety which alone enable civilization to grow.

Therefore, assume peace by power: what then do the young desire?   What kind of life do they propose?   When they speak of walls, they are not envisaging those of a prison. Perhaps, among others, this passage of Trevelyan on Victorian England appeals to them:

Europe, then a world of comparative peace and variegated beauty, not yet mechanized and not yet closed by war and national hatred, was the great playground of the English, who flocked abroad in thousands to spend their newly gotten wealth in exploring the mountains and flower-meadows of Switzerland, the architecture, the galleries, and the landscapes of the Netherlands, Italy and France.   The English traveller of this period took abroad a full mind equipped by some knowledge of history, literature and natural science to observe and appreciate the glory of the world of nature and of man.

If a young man confess that such a passage appeals to him, there will be at once an outcry that such leisurely travelling is a wicked reversion to privilege. All or none! cry the regimenters. Either the whole people must, by right of coupon, go to Rome by state-aided transport-plane, or none shall go! All or none! they cry, and will cry, presumably without great effect, at St. Peter's gate. And there was a time not long ago when the young, smitten by a sickly equalitarian conscience, might have agreed with them. No longer. Cooped as they have been in their regimented island, they have grasped the over-riding truth that social justice is not social sameness, and that to earn one's privilege by matching it with responsibility is not a sin but a virtue. The central crime against a society impoverished as ours has been is by no means to be happier or abler or healthier or more enterprising than other men, but to be a dependent mediocrity, battening upon the State. It may be that the young have no clear answer to the examiner who asks them what kind of society they will have. A faith in blue-prints belongs to an earlier generation than theirs. But it does seem to be true that, unless they are of the kind who expect to have communal shelters built for them, they are reasonably determined to build walls for themselves—of custom, of responsibility, of decorum probably, of principle perhaps, even of privilege—and then, when the bandits are in a cage, to go exploring. Their peril, and so the peril of Western civilization, is that their building may be destroyed by jealous levellers. There is no greater need than the world's need for a creative pause in which men shall have liberty to build and to preserve.

MASTER AND PUPIL
OR
THE LIBERTY OF TEACHING

THOSE of us who have tried to learn but never to teach ought to have more sympathy than we sometimes display with men that are schoolmasters. The simple fact that it is their profession to teach, that they are by definition didactic, lays them open to abuse, particularly in the modern world, where the very word "didactic" is out of favour. This in itself is odd: the world is didactic enough in all conscience; never have more books and pamphlets been written to tell us, with fanatical precision, what to do, how to behave, which queue to stand in and what chorus to shout; and these books and pamphlets are thought to serve a useful purpose. They are said to be "practical" or "vocational" or "instructive" and all these words have a popular, modern sound, particularly when the notion of money-making or of propaganda is associated with them. What makes a schoolmaster suspect is, presumably, that, if he is an honest man, these notions are remote from his didacticism. He is teaching people to think for themselves and to express themselves. He cares more for education, in the word's true and individualistic sense, than for instruction. Therefore he is considered by many to be wasting time.

Yet, of all our schoolmasters, who are they whom we remember with admiration and affection? Never the flat, dutiful, conforming kind, the slaves of a syllabus; never the sleek, the smooth, the soapy with one eye skinned lest the headmaster should walk in; but always the characters, the Landors

of the classroom, who took their own way, who led us off the
map and made it a pride among us not to be uniform, to
excel each in his own way, not to play for safety, not to hide
ourselves in the crowd, above all not to bore them by being
ourselves flat, dutiful and conforming. Some of these men
were tyrants.   No one minded that as long as their wilfulness
remained, in essence, benevolent and warm; it was only when
tyranny became icily sarcastic that it became intolerable, and
small boys, finding that a weapon was being used against
which they had no shield, hardened their hearts with fear, and
could learn no more.   But good schoolmasters, like good
officers, even when they were fierce, seldom used sarcasm for
more than a flick.   It is a stimulus to which free men may
respond, but schoolboys and seamen and soldiers are not
free men; they cannot answer.   Sarcasm is a lash that drives
them into their shells for protection, and it is a schoolmaster's
first duty to persuade a pupil out of his shell.

Among the other characters remembered with honour are
certain men whom we may now think of as " innocents ".   At
first encounter, they who now win that name in our recollection did not seem to be characters at all.   A mild little man
mounted the dais, looked at us shyly and spoke in a gentle
voice.   The tougher members of the class at once assumed
that he was afraid of them and began to ask provocative questions, to drop their books, to spill their ink, to waste time
blatantly, and to make, amid increasingly audible applause,
elaborate experiments in indiscipline.   Suddenly the little
man faced them, not with punishments or the threat of punishments, nor with conciliatory bribes and pleading, but with
one of those plunges deep below the surface of the subject or
one of those excursions far beyond the text-books' range
which are the magic of education.   He quelled the recalcitrant
by enthralling them; he won boys from stupidity by persuading them that they were not stupid; by the leap of his questions

—even more by the gleam of emotion, the hint of excitement and discovery in his asking—he made romantic what had been dull.

A good master teaches first of all that it is a privilege to be taught by him and that what he has to teach is itself an exaltation.   Is it Latin?—then to be in his class is not to grub for notes, as the heathen do in other classes; it is to sup with Catullus, to walk with Virgil, to be received among the civilized.   Is it French?—then to speak it badly is worse than a crime, it is a barbarism, an inelegance, and the boy who can turn a subjunctive or pronounce " *grenouille* " with an R which is not guttural but yet comes softly far away from his anglican teeth is in a fair way to distinguish Romanée Conti from the lesser breeds and to inherit *toutes les gloires de la France*.   Who has forgotten the moment, if ever he experienced it, when, hovering on the outskirts of the calculus, he was enabled to guess what a mathematician is, just as he had guessed one morning what poetry was and had seen all words, as now he saw all figures and symbols, in a radiance of significant order?   Whoever remembers this, though even the foothills of the calculus have since become too steep for him, remembers an expansion of his whole life, an enduring advance in his realization of himself and of the world, and is grateful to the mild little man, the *innocent*, by whom these things came.   He did not know what he had done.   Or did he? Perhaps the great teacher, like the great artist, feels when virtue has gone out of him.

A part of every schoolmaster's life is given to the routine of his class.   He must cover the syllabus; he must not shirk the prescribed books.   However original he himself may be, he is a link in an educational chain and, as such, must do his work faithfully, forbearing so to indulge his originality as to disable the pupil who leaves him from holding his own under a different master or in another school. To this extent he must accept limitations corresponding to those limitations of form which an artist must accept, and the test of his quality is in his power to be neither a slave of those limitations nor a vain rebel against them, but to use them, to inform them with the independence of his spirit, to discover a harmony between the system of which he is a part and the originality of his own ideas. How hard his task is we his pupils may understand in retrospect. Day after day he must face the masked individualities, the armoured reticence of his pupils, and the tendency which every class has to congeal into an impenetrable group. Always he must seek the private mind, must uncover the explosive mixture and drop his spark into it. Even when he succeeds, he may seem to have failed utterly; the detonation is often silent or so long delayed that, when it comes, it is beyond his hearing. Who writes to a master at his preparatory school to say: " It was you who opened Keats for me? " No one, partly because the English male is a shy animal, partly because, in those abrupt and concrete terms, it is seldom quite true.

Rarely can one say with precision which spark lighted the train or where and when it fell. One remembers the man—that he gave out heat and light; one remembers a sense of communication with him and through him; one remembers above all having been emancipated by him from the terrible anonymity of a boy lost in a crowd. With these grateful memories the discovery of Keats or of some other supreme illumination of one's personal life is, perhaps, somehow associated. But how? Where was the point of contact? When did the spark fall? Memory gives no certain answer. Besides, it was long ago. One does not write " fan " letters to preparatory schoolmasters. Mr. Brown has presumably forgotten the scrubby little Smith, aged eleven, who wrote his first essays for him forty years ago. So Mr. Brown, nearing his allotted span now, goes unthanked, except silently, when little Smith clips an adjective or works with a chisel on a relative clause or reads again the Ode that laid his heaven open. " My heart aches, and a drowsy numbness pains my sense. As if . . . as though . . . as if—I'm sorry, sir, I didn't have time to learn it properly." And that morning Mr. Brown said: " Some day you will. Sit down. Listen. It's not ' Repetition '. It's the choirs of heaven." And the boy sat and listened, and his ears were opened and he heard.

Mr. Brown set great store by essays. He was a strict advocate of the classical model and his reasons may be of interest to a reader of what Miss Elizabeth Bowen has written on the subject. So subtle a user of the English language and one so sensitive to its forms and freedoms is to be quoted at length. At the age of twelve she proceeded " from the unalarming ' composition ' to the essay " and found the process embarrassing.

The exclusion of narrative [she says], of out-and-out description and of the word " I " was enjoined. How pathetic were one's class-room attempts at essays, swollen, to the point of elephantiasis, with abstractions, bristling with quotations, callowly didactic! Does the practice of essay-setting persist, in the best schools, still? For really, how hopeless to set very young people to a task which many mature and accomplished writers would prefer not to attempt, or have, anyhow, never successfully achieved!

" Hopeless, indeed," Mr. Brown might have answered, " if what you are looking for in the very young is a masterpiece, but you won't get that anyway, and the classical essay serves well as an exercise—far better, I submit, than a romantic or impressionistic essay could do." To this ghostly comment, unheard by her, Miss Bowen replies:—

The main psychological rule, I suppose, of an essay is that it should be reflective. Young people are not reflective—they are too busy registering impressions; they deal in vivid emotional reflexes.   Reflection implies maturity.   The child and the young person—as, also, a number of people in after-life—only seek for their own reading, and read with genuine pleasure, those essayists who break the schoolroom rules.   These delightful unacademic sinners multiply.   For, since the early nineteenth century, English literature shows an unbroken romantic trend.   The class-room's iron definitions of form show a time-lag.   Progressively the essay has loosened up.

It has indeed.   But Miss Bowen might have added that even in the early eighteenth century, in the heart of the golden age of classicism, Addison, in *The Spectator*, used the pronoun " I ".   He did not use it, as wicked men do now, to vent a personal spite or to reduce an essay to the level of fishwives' gossip, nor as it was used by good men, from Lamb to Walkley, to win grace for their prejudice; but Addison did use it to " loosen up " a sentence as even a dandy may now and then unbutton his coat for an effect of greater ease and, therefore, of greater elegance.   For example, in writing of love, Addison said :—

I have often thought, that there is no way so effectual for the cure of this general infirmity as a man's reflecting upon the motives that produce it.

It is a flawless classical sentence.   The comma after " thought ", the gently ironic choice of the word " infirmity ", the apostrophe-S before " reflecting ", the preferring of " that " to " which " in the final clause, all tell us something of how to put on a coat.   And if the pronoun " I " had been forbidden to Addison, what would have happened then? Why, he would have begun at: " There is no way so effec-tual . . ." and the rule would have been obeyed, the sense have been preserved, and the thin voice of pedantry would have argued that the first five words were proved superfluous.   To this there is an overwhelming answer: that Addison did not think them superfluous, and that Addison was a master. They loosened the top button of his coat; they saved his sentence from being choked in didacticism; they allowed his thought to breathe.   He was not such a fool as to abuse his freedom.   Because he might breathe now and then he did not wildly cast discretion aside and rush through the town with all his egotism flapping in the breezes of gossip and confession. He was Addison; he knew how to write; and to know how to write is to know how to use the English language, and that the first person singular is at once the most dangerous and the most valuable part of it.

Nevertheless, Mr. Brown forbade it in the classroom, and perhaps, in the classroom, he was right.   No one, it is true, ascends Parnassus in a strait-jacket, but the summit was not our immediate destination.   Just as he did not set up Whitman as a model of prosody, so he preferred the classical masters as exemplars of prose.   We were not modelling for an immortal bronze; we were learning how to build an armature, and that a good sentence is not slapped on in plasticine.   Moreover, the stricter the rule within which we worked and the more severe the formal repression of our vague fancies, the more clearly would he be able to discern, in a single, urgent sentence, the pressure of genuine imagination.   His pen would underline it and in the margin would say, not " good " or " very good ", but " queer; where did this come from? "—the one sentence which, while it was being written, had made the writer's hair bristle on his neck.   How did the man know?   Perhaps he would not have known if we had all been little romantics busy with our intimate journals.   He might have lost his way in the too luxuriant forest of " I "s.   As it was, having bound us by rules to which even Addison would not submit, he kept his ears open for the piping of rebellion.   " Where did this come from? "   From where else, in the circumstances, but from inside the pupil himself?

This faculty of looking always " inside the pupil himself ", of drawing him out, of enabling his particular talent and so, in the true sense, of educating him, is an admitted virtue in tutors; indeed, all that is best in the system of our great universities springs from it; but it is a virtue less recognized in humbler schoolmasters, and for them, sometimes, bitterly hard to practise.   In the future it will be harder, and hard even in the universities themselves.   The more reason that we should honour it where it is found and do what we may in the coming world to combat those tendencies which, unchecked, would make it impossible.

Of these, some—the large class, the habit of adjusting the speed of the convoy to that of the slowest ship, and the bleak pressure of utilitarianism—are well-recognized evils; only high policy can hope to find a remedy for them.   But there are other threats to the personal relationship of master and pupil which we, whose influence on educational policy is exceedingly remote, may by questioning and sympathy, above all by being selective in our demands, do a little to mitigate. The necessary questions are awkward ones.   What precisely do we understand by the " team spirit "?   How much shall we be impressed by the schoolmaster who has that nobly sounding phrase for ever on his lips?   The worship of it may be a curse upon individuality.   It is not sacred; it is open to question; let us question it.   Linked with it is the problem of compulsory games.   Even one who happened to excel in them may remember with hatred their pretentiousness, the hypocrisy of athlete-worship which they imposed, the false hierarchy they set up, the applause and sycophancy they required, their wasting of precious hours.   There is another point of view, but let us at least ask whether, in a world that will require more and more of master and pupil, their hours outside the class-room are best given to the organization and performance of this everlasting drill.   May they not go for a walk in the country or read or idle or think or sleep? May they not choose? It is the word " compulsory " that stings. The compelled games may be good for the health or, as some claim, good for morals, but they are a recent incubus; health and morals survived their absence through many centuries; and to thousands of boys they are a reasonless tyranny. To question them will by many be considered heretical, but we must be prepared for a little heresy if the conditions of the coming world are not to raise up between master and pupil barriers that neither has the spirit to penetrate.

OLD KASPAR'S WORK UNDONE
OR
THE LIBERTY TO HAVE ROOTS

A MAN whose age is now in the neighbourhood of fifty and who is, therefore, a survivor of what has been called the Lost Generation, was inclined a few years ago to be a little resentful of the name, which seemed to imply his exclusion from the affairs of the world; but the name is no longer current, the accompanying resentment has become meaningless, and he is able to reflect with a certain detachment upon his peculiar state. It may be questioned whether he should reflect upon it at all as being peculiar, for to think in age-groups is a vague and dangerous way of thought; and yet his age-group is so clearly defined and so islanded by the chances of recent history that it has at least the interest of being unique. Though all lives are transitional the pace of transition varies and in his half-century has been extreme. Not only this, but his half-century began at the end of an epoch—an end so heavily under-scored with mental and mechanical changes that, even at the time, its finality was recognized by those who witnessed it. There were few in England outside the cradle who did not feel that the death of Queen Victoria was the death of more than a Sovereign, and as cradles themselves went into mourning on that occasion even their occupants may have noticed the general dark. Now, of those who rocked Victorian cradles, few remain, and many who were children at their first school when the reign ended fell in battle a quarter of a century ago. Victoria died on 22 January 1901—the anniversary, an irrelevant memory recalls, of Lord Byron's and of Strindberg's births. Ruskin and Wilde had died in the preceding year.

Rhodes and Samuel Butler were still alive, and " Kim " was about to come from the press. England was at war. Soon those who have personal recollection of any of these things or of the fact of being alive at that time will be exceedingly rare animals. A surviving member of the Lost Generation, particularly if he be male, will have become an almost prehistoric beast with his clear though childish memories of the Victorian age.

His fortune has been unusual. After the Four Years War, in the eyes of his younger contemporaries, he grew old suddenly at the age of about twenty-five. In the early months of the war that had ended war he had committed the absurdity of going into action with a pistol in one hand and a sword in the other, or perhaps even upon a horse. His younger contemporaries had at the time been emerging from the nursery, and by 1919 his sword was for them a battle-axe; in their debating societies they passed resolutions to that effect. Mr. Coward was twenty; the world was new. Nothing remotely resembling what had happened would ever happen again. Experience itself had become an anachronism. With two score years and five stretching before him, Old Kaspar's work was done. His conviction that it was being undone and would have to be done again was considered a part of his old-fashioned prejudice. The nature of that prejudice and the group of values in which it originated may be worth examining for other than antiquarian reasons. There may spring up in the near future a body of opinion eager to undo what is now being done for a second time.* Experience may again become an anachronism—and it is improbable that a third time will be lucky.

Old Kaspar, it will be recalled, was born within range of

* First published in *The Times Literary Supplement* 22 May, 1943. Particularly for the sake of its conclusion, this essay has been left untouched.

that St. Valentine's Day of 1895 on which *The Importance of Being Earnest* appeared at the St. James's Theatre. Unless he belonged to an exceptional family, his nursery was neither Whistlerian nor Japanese, and not until he discovered it for himself in later years was he aware of the æsthetic revolt. The pictures on his walls were predominantly royal or martial, his pianos were upright and backed with silk, his fairy stories were Grimm and unpotted, his soldiers wore scarlet, the women of his family were Tennyson's, though he, and perhaps they, knew it not. His cook was by Dickens, his governess by Thackeray, and his vicar's wife by Burne-Jones. He sang hymns (and not in church only) with more than formal ardour, and he smelt, and seemed afterwards to remember, the smell of Diamond Jubilee bonfires. In the country, he went out to hay-parties in the summer, and at Christmas-time to rare and dazzling feasts of sugar-cake and white muslin and glossy slippers and candle-light, reached, when snowdrifts did not sink the wheels, in a carriage whose leathered stuffiness was an odour of festivity and whose lamps drew magical ribbons across the icy fir and bramble of narrow lanes. These were the decorations of Old Kaspar's little decorated childhood. School was bleakly austere and fiercely competitive. To fall a place in the weekly order, not to advance a class in the terminal promotion, was to lose—and, it seemed then, to lose for ever—advancement in the race of life itself. For what was rubbed into Old Kaspar from the cradle, or at any rate from the cot, was a sense of continuity, of life's being, in this world and the next, an unbroken chain of cause and consequence. As he sowed, so he should reap— the penalty or the reward. Already, at each instant of his life, the grain was flying from his hand. Never, sleeping or waking, was he irresponsible, and the responsibility, on the whole, pleased more than it troubled him, for it gave to his life the three supreme blessings: meaning, liberty and order.

All of them depended upon the security of his background—that is to say, of his parents' home, of the home he would some day build for himself, and of his country.

The Victorians were by no means aggressive, but they had a quality, in their public and their private lives, which is now so rare, so remote, so hard to refer to any yard-stick of our own experience, that it may easily be mistaken for aggressiveness or at least for arrogance.   This quality, for which there is no single name, had two aspects: seen from one angle it was complacency—a sense of having inexhaustible reserves, the men, the ships, " the money too "; seen from another angle, it was stability—a stability so profound that the great bulk of Victorian society was much less affected by doubt and Darwinism than the more articulate memoirs lead us to suppose, and Fabianism, like illicit love, troubled few except those who were looking for trouble.   This stability was the result of long experience.   There had been wars, scandals, controversy, angry debates; the Victorians themselves were far from believing that their lives had been lived in one of history's least agitated periods; but in fact the wars, the scandals and the controversies, however dangerously they had struck underground, had not broken up the order of their living, and to prevent that break-up they were willing to make great efforts and great sacrifices.   Sacrifices of everything—stoical sacrifices of their own comfort in order " to keep up appearances ", elaborate sacrifices of minor conscience in order that what were regarded as the major demands of conscience might be satisfied, heroic sacrifices of parents for children, of the present for the future, of enjoyment for duty—all for the warding off of any threat to that stability which, though not life itself, was for them the springboard of endeavour.   Nothing in them is to be understood without understanding first of all that conservation and progress were interlocked and interdependent in their minds.   The history of Gladstone and Disraeli has its key

in this.   To those coming after who have not the key, Gladstone may appear as a pompous conservative mouthing radicalism, Disraeli as a fantastic self-contradiction in imperialism
and reform, and both as hypocrites; but hypocrite is a dangerous word to use of any man, and most dangerous of the
Victorians, whose whole ideal rested upon their belief that
stability and ordered change were interdependent.   How
could you climb a mountain if the earth was crumbling beneath
your feet?

By 22 January 1901 much of the ground was, in fact,
crumbling—had crumbled deep down, but the surface held.
It was a sense of inner disintegration, of something failing and
weakening, which emphasized the shock of the Queen's death.
Next morning, *The Times*, having referred to the " enormous
social and economic progress " and the " moral and spiritual
improvement " which had marked the reign, struck this
ominous note:—

> It is also true, unfortunately, that the impetus has to some extent
> spent itself.   At the close of the reign we are finding ourselves
> somewhat less secure of our position than we could desire, and
> somewhat less abreast of the problems of the age than we ought
> to be.

The direct reference was to trade and the application of
science to it, but there were many other departments of life
in which the Late Victorians were finding themselves somewhat
less secure of their position than they could desire.   In religion,
for example, and in the matters of property and sex.   *Industrial
Democracy* had appeared in 1897, *Plays Pleasant and Unpleasant* in 1898, *The Psychology of Sex* in 1899; it was a
disturbing succession.   It has also to be remembered—though
certainly Old Kaspar cannot remember it—that two or three
decades earlier the Victorians' mountain had been shaken by
internal upheavals of their own making.   While increasing

the complexity of society and of the problems it had to solve, they had, in their enthusiasm for representative democracy, diluted the influence of their most judicial minds.   Mr. G. M. Young, in his *Portrait of an Age*, made this clear.   " In a limited electorate, the educated classes still counted as a body; and science, fast as it was growing, was not yet either so extensive or minute that its achievements could not be followed and borne in mind."

The public which bought 100,000 copies of the *Cornhill* when Thackeray was editor, supported the stout quarterlies and paid toll to the proprietor of the *Athenæum* at a rate of £7,000 a year clear profit, was, if not a well-informed public, at least a public that desired to take care of its mind, a public trained in the keen debates of the Oxford and Free Trade movements, and ready to act as jury if not judge in any controversy that might arise in future. But by successive stages, in 1867 and 1885, the educated class was disfranchised, while the advance of the arts and sciences was withdrawing them from the observation and practice of the individual educated man.

The result was that the educated Late Victorians—or those of them who saw clearly what was happening—felt that, though they might still be on the box, the reins and the whip were slipping from their hands and civilization was in danger of bolting.   They were, and knew they were, in the early stages of that process which we have carried to its logical conclusion. New problems were coming up for decision; the former jury were " disfranchised " or, strictly, swamped by a vast enfranchisement; and the new problems were precisely those upon which an untrained democracy was least capable of adjudicating.   At the same time, as the Late Victorians saw, the old religious loyalties were weakening.   For lack of them new medicine-men and new fetiches would be raised up. " Where shall we look," Mr. Young has asked,

for the successors of the Mills and Ruskins and Tennysons?   Or of the public for which they wrote?   The common residual intelligence is becoming impoverished for the benefit of the specialist, the technician and the æsthete . . . and through the gate-way of the Competitive Examination we go out into the Waste Land of Experts, each knowing so much about so little that he can neither be contradicted nor is worth contradicting.

It is true of us, and the late Victorians knew that it was becoming true of them. They may not have foreseen a day in which the trade of the world might depend on questions of currency incomprehensible to the electorates who must ultimately answer them, or the peace of the world on European or Asiatic treaties unenforceable except by the consent of mass-industries and mass-armies uninformed on foreign affairs; but they were aware of the danger in which they stood and knew that they were " somewhat less abreast of the problems of the age than they ought to be ".

But they were still courageously self-reliant. Believing, as we still believe, that representative democracy could in the end by adjustment, compromise, patience and education be released from its executive disabilities, they preferred, as we still prefer, the logical defects of that system, which was at any rate human and flexible, to the steely inhumanity of dic-tatorships. They were determined, as we are, to go on with their great democratic experiment and to make it work, but they felt an anxiety which *The Times* expressed :—

The " condition of England question " does not present itself in so formidable a shape as at the beginning of the reign, but it does arouse the attention of those who try to look a little ahead of current business.

In brief, anxious though they might be, they were very far from throwing up their hands and saying (as we are in danger of saying): " The pace is too fast, the problem too large for us! The Government and the Experts will provide!" Though Late, they were still Victorians. They were respon-sible. If they worked and thought and sacrificed themselves, reform might still draw its strength from an essential stability.

They were responsible, in their public or their private lives, for their country, their government, their families, and, it may be remembered, for their souls.   With this sense of responsibility, their love of the voluntary system in all things was closely linked.   Their lives were their own to make or mar; their collective life, fast though it was changing, was not to be thought of as having passed beyond their control.   Though they might hold neither whip nor reins, they might yet influence the use of them and prevent civilization from taking the bit between its teeth.   Among these people, Old Kaspar spent those early years of his existence in which, wise men have said, character receives its shape.

But character is made partly by absorption from an environment and partly by revolt against it.   The consequence is that Old Kaspar and his Lost Generation are themselves by no means Victorians, having revolted strongly against their parents' abnormally developed sense of family and against many another principle or convention of that anxious and yet self-confident age.   But Old Kaspar has inherited from his childhood certain notions of conduct and policy which, though they made him appear old-fashioned in the twenty years following 1919, may not be inapplicable to the conditions that will follow the present war.*   It is the custom of the young to throw back beyond their immediate predecessors, and it may well happen that those who inherit what remains of the earth in 1950 may feel themselves to be in some respects less remote from him who fought the war of 1914 than from those by whom his work was undone.   For what the world will need above all else is time in which to be healed—that is to say, stability as a basis of reform, and this is a requirement with which Old Kaspar has a natural sympathy and for which he is willing to pay.   The young may be a little sceptical of their

* See footnote, p. 133.

more urgent guides and say, in their own language, what Old Kaspar learned from the Victorians: that the two certain ways of failing to reach a summit are, first, to destroy the mountain; and, secondly, to sit down in a pool of disillusioned self-pity and wonder why the funicular railway, which all the ideologists promised, has not begun to run.

THE GLOW OF LIVING
OR
LIBERTY IN TIME

THERE is such a thing as an inverted historical imagination. It can be an agony and a delight. Today, in February,* the fourth of the five months of winter-endurance, and the sixth February of war, we have great need of it; for now endurance is hardest, the strength of summer and the tranquillity of autumn have gone out of us, and there is long to wait even for the almond. The present is bleak and heartless. We must feel ourselves to be historical beings, for, if we do not, when we stretch out our hands to the fire of life, it does not glow.

Must " feel "—not think only. In the plain study of history there is a distinction, which historians know, between historical judgement and historical imagination or feeling. They overlap, they run together and contribute to each other, as prose overlaps with poetry or friendship with love, but there is a clear distinction between them. Historical judgement enables a reader to know and estimate the past, to understand it as one whose centre of life is outside it; so a traveller may understand a country of which he is not native or a house that is not his home. Historical imagination enables a reader not only to see the past but to be of it, to understand it from the inside outwards as though he had been born in it, to feel what it was to be alive then. Without a fusing in him of these two qualities of the historical power a historian is vulnerable to his prejudices. If his judgement only is strong, he may be betrayed into using it to plead a modern and irrelevant

* First published, *T.L.S.*, 3 February 1945. Deliberately untouched.

cause; and if his imagination, his gift of self-identification with a living past, is greatly stronger than his judgement, he may lose in perspective more than he gains by intimacy.

That this is true of our " inverted " sense of history is not ordinarily remarked.   Students are rightly told that historical study is a valuable training for the conduct of their own lives. It broadens and deepens their judgement; it lends perspective to their view of contemporary affairs; and—though this is less often said—it tempers their enthusiasm.   Thus a historian's quality of judgement may, when inverted in us, enable us to look back upon our own times from the point of view of men as yet unborn, and an attempt to do this is sometimes made in these essays.   Much less often do we " invert " the other quality of a historian, his power of self-identification with the past.   This, if " inverted ", would enable us imaginatively to convert the present into a historical period; we should feel ourselves to be living not on the outermost edge of time's flow, not as extreme bubbles on a rising tide, but within history itself, within the tide, the future having, as it were, flowed over and beyond us.

Before anyone decides that this is avoidance or " escapism ", it will be better to consider the idea farther, for what is implied in it is, in fact, the opposite of " escapism ".   To avoid, to escape from life is to run away from the sea and hide in a cave; to perform the act of inverted historical imagination is, indeed, not to stand, where the self-called realists insist on standing, in the surf, wet and exposed, paddling, buffeted and complaining, but to plunge into the sea, beyond the surf, and to swim.   It is an act, not of cowardice and avoidance, but of reason and penetration.   That it carries the swimmer into calmer water beyond the breakers is not a reason to condemn it.   Nevertheless it is unquestionably a form of romanticism. It is that form of penetrative romanticism which the future holds, in life and literature, as an alternative to a barren and deliberately superficial materialism.

The idea of inverted historical imagination is best made clear in a simple and crude example of its working. The example is, in itself, so crude and trivial that it invites the ridicule of any who wish to ridicule it; that risk may be willingly accepted in an attempt to be clear at all costs. The crude example is this: On 3 February 1945 a woman at the end of her day's work is reading at her fireside. Her attention wanders from her book and she lays it down. Her thought is discontinuous—a series of scattered images and anxieties. There is no good thing to which she looks back except with a sense of irreplaceable loss; there is nothing to which she looks forward with confidence and pleasure. She blames herself for this. She knows that she can break away from this condition of mind by continuous work, by serving others and serving her country, and that tomorrow she will in fact liberate herself by this means; but she knows also that, whenever the anodyne of action is withheld, this condition of mind returns, and, though she is not personally unhappy or self-pitying, she feels as if the present were a distracted brain and as if she were living inside one of its cells.

But if she should by chance reflect that the dress she wears is, from the point of view of a generation hence, a historical costume; that the open fire in her grate and the way in which she does her hair will soon seem as remote as a sedan-chair and powder; if she remembers that the new book she has just laid down is also the first edition of a very old one; if she remembers that someone will say, " How impossible it is to imagine oneself living on the 3rd of February, 1945," and that she is living through that remote evening and hearing the tick of its clock; then she will no longer feel that her life is included in the cell of a maddened brain, for actuality will have begun to be for her translucent. The present is not felt to be insane unless it solidifies in the mind and becomes opaque and rigid; then to live in it is to live among bricks in an earth-quake. But if the woman seated at her fireside, beginning from the trivial thought that her dress is a historical costume, should continue the process of inverted historical imagination, she may fluidify the present so that it becomes, not fragmented, brittle, disordered, but an instant in a continuous flow. She may reach the condition of feeling what it *was* like to have been alive during the evening of 3 February 1945.

All this, it may seem for a moment, amounts to no more than to provide a morbid woman with a fanciful escape from her morbidity. It might be no more if she went no farther. Certainly it is no remedy for men's suffering that they should romanticize themselves as performers in a costume play. Nevertheless, the idea itself is seminal. The woman is exercising, in an elementary form, an imaginative power which, if it is developed and rightly applied, may correct and vitalize her judgement of her own life and of contemporary affairs, just as a historian's imaginative self-transfer into the past may correct and vitalize his judgement of it.

In the handling of certain manuscripts one may receive a hint of this power. During the war, in New York, an English lady was a guest in the house of the owner of a great private library. After dinner she was seated on a sofa in a room shelved from floor to ceiling and full of precious things. Her host moved about behind her, taking down for her inspection books of which he was proud, and particularly—for he had the special imaginative courtesy of American hosts—those which he thought might please or comfort her by proving his love for her own country. He had plenty from which to choose. Few of his books were " rare " only in the sense of their being first editions of which other copies might be found elsewhere. Nearly all of them were made unique by association: if you took *Treasure Island* from its case you found that it had been inscribed by Stevenson as a gift to his mother. The English lady examined, and talked to her host about, each book shown to her, and while their conversation, and the conversation of others in the room, continued, treasures accumulated at her side. Then, saying nothing as he leaned over her shoulder, her host dropped in her lap a piece of manuscript. Continuing to turn the pages of the book already in her hand, and to talk of it, she did not at first observe the newcomer. Then she picked it up—listlessly, another treasure to be admired!—and began to read. She was silent, and with a silence so intense that the whole company was affected by it. Chatter ceased. It was as though she were passing through some deep personal experience, as though she herself were suffering and the world respected her suffering. When she had read perhaps a dozen or twenty lines, she raised her head, sought her host, handed the paper to him. " But have you read it? " She shook her head silently. " I can't. It wasn't meant for me." It was a letter of Keats.

The imagination she had exercised was, strictly, the historical imagination; she had felt what it was to be alive on the day and at the hour in which the letter was written, had seen the hand move across the page and felt the outward pressure of the pen on the holding fingers. Who will may say disapprovingly that she had " romanticized " Keats—a sin that shall be forgiven her. But whether or not she was allowing her historical imagination to run away with her is not at present the point. The point is that, in exercising, she also inverted it; in feeling what it was to dip a pen and write those words, she began to feel also what it was to *have been* alive, as an Englishwoman, in New York during the spring of 1941; and when her host had taken the manuscript from her and she turned again to the room full of people, she was at peace in her mind, she was moving in the full tide of history, not buffeted in the shallows of doubt and controversy. A serenity came to her, and her imagination cooled and fortified her judgement. When her eye fell on a copy of the *New York Times* lying on a long stool before the fireplace, she read its date almost with curiosity; its headlines, which were alarming enough, ceased to daunt her. Fortune was not breaking over her head, for she was in the flow of it.

Those who are inclined to say that this notion of our attempting to exercise an inverted historical imagination is extremely fine-drawn, artificial and unpractical seem at first to have reason on their side. To indicate what the idea is has been difficult, and if an honest reader has wondered now and then whether he was being called upon to read Henry James backwards, he has the writer's active sympathy. Nevertheless, however hard it may be to expound the idea, the practical application of it is plain enough. Shakespeare applied it continually, and nowhere more plainly than on the field of Agincourt, where the King, to put heart into his followers when they found themselves challenged and out-numbered, compelled them to see their perilous instant as a particle in the flow of time:

> He that outlives this day, and comes safe home,
> Will stand a tip-toe when this day is named,
> And rouse him at the name of Crispian.

It is much more than a promise of future honours. It is a command to see the day itself as being already historical. Nor is it necessary to go back to the fifteenth century for plain instances. Evidently the exercise of an inverted historical imagination cannot be reserved to Jamesian specialists, for all England exercised it after the collapse of France in 1940, and it is our relative failure to exercise it now that makes the living of life harder than it was then. Then what gave England the virtue which so suddenly appeared in her and was communicated by some miracle of communication (and not by propaganda) to the watching world; what gave her not only courage, which was to be expected of her, but a wonderful serenity and lightness of heart brilliantly contrasted with the barren greyness of the preceding months and years, was precisely that men and women—not Jamesians only but all except a few totalitarians and avid, conciliatory tradesmen— knew in their hearts what it was to *have been alive* in the weeks through which they were then living. There is a sense in which it is certainly true to say that they dramatized and romanticized their own lives, and little men hereafter will write books and plays to show how self-deluded the English were during that summer and how much cleverer they would have been if . . . But that is of no account; we shall not be there to read the books or sit through the plays. What we may now be sure of is that, if the English were deluded then, if they then dramatized and romanticized themselves, it was their delusions that saved them and redeemed their reputation in the world.

Perhaps men ought to be able to live on the flat statistics of existence, on a close reckoning of profit and loss, but they cannot. If they try, not only do they collaborate with external enemies but with the enemy that is within themselves. A life which is not imagined while it is being lived becomes existence merely. Purpose is not enough; even an ideal which can be counted and weighed is not enough to prevent that existence from becoming drab and brittle. That is why a society destroys itself which succeeds in persuading its men and women that they live, not in themselves, but as members of it. And if we would imagine our lives while we live them, we must see them not as the ticking of a tape-machine, but as a story in which we believe because it is a story. " This story shall the good man teach his son."

That process of mind, to which, at the outset, the awkwardly sounding name of "inverted historical imagination" was reluctantly given, appears, then, to be after all simple enough. You say to yourself that this third day of February is a historical date and that you are a historical character, and the trick appears to be done. But if that were all, it would be no more than a trick, and valueless. It is not enough to say this and think it; it is necessary to imagine it, to feel it to be true, to enter into the truth of it. Without this, it is no more than fancifulness and empty pretence—romanticism in the corrupt sense of falsification. Just as a historian, who tries to project himself into the past, achieves nothing better than costume-drama if his self-projection is merely decorative and fanciful, so we play our trick to no good purpose if we go no farther than thinking of our clothes, our social habits, the trappings of our lives. Then we are but playing the childish game of dressing up, and are not entering imaginatively into the continuous human tragi-comedy; we are theatricalizing, not genuinely dramatizing ourselves.

In the noblest sense, the English dramatized themselves in the summer of 'Forty, and, seeing that the play was a great one—the same that Shakespeare wrote for the stage and Hardy for the library—they played their part, saved from doubt and swerving by their self-loss in it, ringed in as actors are by the glorious and all-excluding light of their everlasting world. It appeared to them not as a warlike drama only. Being full of lyrics, it was *As You Like It* much more truly than it was *Henry V*; it was epic, too, a great morality, Milton had a hand in it. All the poetry of England was in each man's plain action; his action glowed; and suddenly he was happy and she invincible. Was that romanticism? Perhaps, but it was truth, like Gray's sunrise: " I saw the clouds and dark vapours open gradually to right and left, rolling over one another in great smoky wreaths . . . and all at once a little line of insufferable brightness that (before I can write these five words) was grown to half an orb, and now to a whole one, too glorious to be distinctly seen.   It is very odd it makes no figure on paper; yet I shall remember it as long as the sun, or at least as long as I endure.   I wonder whether anybody ever saw it before?   I hardly believe it."

THE WINE AND THE BOTTLE
OR
THE LIBERTY TO ENJOY AND ACCEPT

It must have been some thirty years ago, at the end of the first German war, that my own contemporaries listened for the first time to that little company of wise and foolish men —Remenham, the Liberal Prime Minister; Reuben Mendoza, his Conservative rival; Wilson, Allison and the rest—whose discussion of life and politics and progress was recorded by Lowes Dickinson in *A Modern Symposium*. The book had, indeed, appeared in 1905, but we had been in Eton collars during that epoch of surviving civilization, and it was not for another dozen years or more that the dialogue came our way. Its grace and honesty, its determination to get to the bottom of things, were apparent; it became a treasured book, but rather, it must be confessed, as a work of art than as a close comment upon our own lives. We were at the moment in our early twenties; we were alive, a little to our astonishment; we were discovering Plato himself, and what with the *Phædo* and the spring and our own new world were disinclined to take Remenham and Mendoza as mentors. Nevertheless, being wise youths, we permitted in ourselves the instinct of the squirrel, with the consequence that today the volume comes down from its shelf with—well, almost with a smile at our expense, but not with an ungenerous one.

It is too patient, above all too courteous to say: " I told you so," but, like all enduring books, opens itself and waits. " Perhaps, however," one of the protagonists is saying, " before proceeding to analyse the spiritual ideals of the American people, I had better give some account of their

country," and the ensuring discussion reverberates from
Georgia to Grosvenor Square.   Or there is the ultimate
scepticism of Audubon, the man of business, who has " no
clue to the enigma you seem so lightly to solve by your
religion, your philosophy, your science ", and who says out-
right that though there may be, beyond the waters in which
we are shipwrecked, a harbour, he cannot steer for it, having
" no rudder, no compass, no chart ".   This is an extreme
counter to the varying doctrines of progress that others have
advanced, and is a valuable challenge to vague complacency—
a reminder that, if we would refute despair, we cannot do
so by brightly dismissing it, but have a responsibility (which
has not lightened since 1905) to discover an alternative and
establish it at least within ourselves.   But of all the views
represented in *A Modern Symposium* that which touches us
most nearly is, perhaps, Coryat's.   It is important today for
two reasons: first, that it is seldom expressed and asserts a
valuation of life which has become uncommonly hard;
secondly, that our later experience may both endorse and
qualify what Coryat said in 1905.

What he said may be summarized as a recommendation to
mankind to count its benefits and pass the wine, which—let
us add swiftly—is by no means the same thing as a recommendation to gather rosebuds.   The purposeful gathering of
rosebuds is a greedy and faithless activity, and Coryat was
neither faithless nor greedy.   The value of him is, precisely,
that he was not panic-stricken, and treated the present calmly
as a thing precious in itself, a road open to sunlight, not a
thin alley between the walls of past and future.   He liked his
journey and said so:—

For my part, I find life extraordinarily good, just as it is, not
mine only, I mean, but everybody's—

a saying which, if made today in most companies, would call
down a storm of protest.   But Coryat's remarks have to be

read in their context.   He is not denying the evil of life, but he is denying that the evil excludes the good:—

Of course the things really are bad that you say are bad.   But they're so good as well.

Man—the instance he gives is the agricultural labourer—is not " an incarnate grievance ".

I don't mean you aren't right to worry, in a way; except that no one ought to worry.   But you oughtn't to suppose it's all a dreadful and intolerable thing, just because you can imagine something better. . . . I'm not saying people are happy. . . . But anyhow they are interested.   And that interest is perennial, and of all ages and all classes.   And if you leave it out, you leave out the only thing that counts.

The great river of life, he says, is itself its own justification, and a community which does not realize this is incapable of receiving and enjoying what social reform may give them:—

Their last state may even be worse than the first, because they will have lost the natural instinctive acceptance of life, without learning how to accept it on the higher plane.

" Acceptance " is the key-word—a word which nowadays is often an occasion of reproof.   There are men who think that it is synonymous with resignation to evil and that whoever uses it desires nothing better of life than to sit all day in the devil's parlour and twiddle his thumbs.   Will he not, they ask, be up and doing?   Will he not look with them through the window of the future and contemplate the Promised Land? But this is to beg the question.   Of course, unless he is Audubon, he will look through the window and rejoice in whatever light falls through it; but that it contains windows, looking out to future and past, is not a reason for speaking of the present house of life as a hovel: on the contrary, it is a means of seeing it and accepting it.   Acceptance is not resignation or despair; it is a receiving of life, a refusal to discountenance what is good in it because, as Coryat said, we can, or believe we can, imagine something better.

It has become more and more a habit of mind to classify men by their attitudes towards past and future—to say, if their eyes are bent upon the past, that they are " reactionary " and, if upon the future, that they are " revolutionary ".   It is astonishingly believed that, in varying degrees, all men must belong to one category or the other, and we attach accordingly politer names to the more moderate past-gazers and future-gazers, calling them conservatives or progressives or what we will, for all the world as if there were no other objects of a reasonable man's gazing but the future and the past.   What about the present? Coryat would say.   After all, we live in it and shall never live in anything else.   To care for it and " accept " it for what it is worth, not only does not exclude the hope of an improved future but is, in fact, a condition of our being able to benefit by improvement when it comes.

Here, it would seem, is a sharer of the belief which I have already advanced *: that there is nothing anti-social, nothing selfish or blind, in discovering here and now *la douceur de vivre*.   Hitherto *la douceur* has been upheld, as a quality of the present, against those who, like Talleyrand, are inclined to see it only in the past.   Coryat reminds us that it has as much to be upheld against those who see it only in the future —the obsessed future-gazers who, in loyalty to their obsession, think of the past as a long and bitter failure and of the present as being always out-of-date.

There must, I am sure [says Coryat], be something wrong about a view that makes the past and the present merely a means to the future.   It's as though one were to take a bottle and turn it upside down, emptying the wine out without noticing it; and then plan how tremendously one will improve the shape of the

* *Reflections in a Mirror* (First Series).

bottle. Well, I'm not interested in the shape of bottles. And I am interested in wine. And—which is the point—I know that the wine is always there. It was there in the past, it's here in the present, and it will be there in the future; yes, in spite of all of you!

Is not this a test that may well be applied to planners? The catchword is used so often, so loosely, so arrogantly, that there is a temptation to rebel against it, but we must neither rebel against catchwords as such nor accept them as such. We are to shun the prejudice of words and seek always their significance on the lips that use them. Is the man (or the party or the organization) who claims to plan our future interested in the blue-print for its own sake—in the shape of the bottle? Or is he able to taste the wine and eager that mankind shall taste it? *A Modern Symposium* has opened itself at a passage that has grown more rather than less urgent since Coryat spoke.

Two later speakers, an aristocrat and a Quaker, criticized Coryat, on the ground that he " seemed to think that any and all life is good ". The aristocrat, Harington, claimed that it was wrong to assume, as nearly all the company had assumed, that " the good life, whatever it may be, can be obtained by everybody "; on the contrary, it could be obtained, as in Greece, only by the few; in thinking otherwise the democracies were debasing life by averaging it, were lowering the standard of goodness itself and abandoning true greatness for the sake of justice and mediocrity; and he said that Coryat's " undistinguishing approval of life " was as much out of place as Audubon's undistinguishing censure. The Quaker, Woodman, accused Coryat of having failed to see the line between the children of God and the children of this world. But Coryat seems, if we study his words, to be little deserving of their strictures. It is true that he did not make the distinctions they demand, but nowhere did he deny them, nor is denial implicit in his speech. To the general cry of: " Wine yesterday!" and "Wine tomorrow!" he responded by passing the decanter. That is by no means to say that he failed to discriminate among vintages. His case, as it appears to us, was much stronger than his critics would allow, and might be further strengthened by the amendments that our experience would suggest.

His argument is chiefly vulnerable in his saying that he found everybody's life "extraordinarily good, just as it is". This, if strictly interpreted, is untrue. It is not true, even, that everyone's life is dear to him. A physical instinct of self-preservation endures; a man who sees that he is about to be run over by a cart will avoid it if he can; but this does not prevent its being true that there are many on earth who have ceased to care, in the leisure of reason, whether they wake up tomorrow morning. It is probable that during the last forty years their number has increased, but they existed in Coryat's day, and it was unquestionably false to say of them, and of many others who had not reached their condition of indifference or despair, that their life was "extraordinarily good". But that Coryat, in order to arrest his listeners' attention, over-stated his case at the outset does not vitiate it. What he should have said and what he did, in effect, say afterwards is that there is in life a present and essential goodness which is itself independent of the accidents of fortune, though the accidents of fortune may render a man incapable of "accepting" it—that is, of receiving it into his consciousness. But these accidents of fortune are not always, are indeed very seldom, accidents of material condition. Life does not become tasteless because a man is poor or is persecuted or is engulfed in war; it never becomes tasteless; it becomes untastable by men who have lost the faculty of tasting, and this loss of faculty, though material conditions of poverty or persecution or war may contribute to it, is a disease of the spirit by which

the free or the rich may be stricken and from which the poor
and the persecuted may be exempt.

If this may be accepted as a restatement of Coryat's argument, our own experience is seen at once to endorse it.   Since
he spoke, disaster after disaster has befallen mankind.   To say
that everybody's life is " extraordinarily good " has become
ridiculous if, in saying it, we are thinking in terms of those
things which Coryat's friends had in mind when they spoke of
progress.   What was to them the future has in fact been a
steady movement towards barbarism interrupted by ineffectual
idealistic swerves.   Yet the extreme misfortunes by which
men and women have been visited—the loss of their homes,
their friends and their possessions—have by no means made
them " incarnated grievances ".   They have not so regarded
themselves in England or even, if the evidences of resistance
have meaning, in countries partly or wholly overrun by a
foreign horde.   The lesson of the twentieth century has been
again and again that men whose whole existence has been over-
thrown and who, whatever the fortunes of war, have little to
hope for in the future, have been capable of an " acceptance "
of life which is altogether distinct from resignation to the evil
in it.   Mankind seems to have discovered in itself an extraordinary steadfastness of which courage is only a part—a
steadfastness of the spirit, an acceptance of life even as it now
is, which could not have endured so long if the taste of an
essential good in being alive had been lost.   What seems to
have happened is that, the surface of existence having become
dry and barren, men, almost in proportion to the degree of
their suffering, have dug deep within themselves for the spring
of life.   Woodman, the Quaker, might have said that the
children of this world had been driven to discover that they
were inhabited by the children of light.

If this is true, it is true also that the necessity from which it has sprung has imposed a great strain upon man. Where he has survived he has survived by living, so to speak, on his spiritual capital, of which—often to his own astonishment— he has unearthed great treasures. If he is of deep religious conviction, he will not be alarmed lest this capital exhaust itself; he will believe that by Grace it will be renewed; but this is the twentieth century, it is not an age of faith, and it is not inconceivable that the steadfastness of man might break, his power of acceptance be exhausted, and he at last cry out with Audubon's despair: " I have no rudder, no compass, no chart. . . . And the best for which I can hope is speedily to be lost in the silent gulf of oblivion." The danger is real—so real and so evident that future-gazers can nearly always do a brisk trade in rudders, compasses and charts. A thousand busy boats swarm about man, the shipwrecked mariner cling- ing to his spar, and a thousand voices urge him to new invest- ments of spiritual capital in the voyages they recommend. " Push my boat," one cries. " I will set the course and soon we shall come to the Promised Land." " Set my sail," another insists. " Beyond the horizon are the Isles of the Blest! " Always beyond the horizon. . . . Who, meanwhile, will lift the shipwrecked mariner out of the water and let him rest and give him wine? To allow him to rest, to re-order his affairs, to re-acquire what he has so nearly lost—a sense of continuity— may be the greatest service that can be offered to him and, in the long view, the greatest to progress.

The argument has swung full-circle. We are back to Coryat again. If future-gazers are to be prevented from treating man as an incarnate grievance and wearing him out with their remedies, it will be necessary to insist that life is worth living and not merely worth hoping for. Insistence cannot take the form of pretending that all is for the best in the best of all possible worlds, for the shipwrecked mariner is not a fool and he will not believe it. Nor, being without a

pagan education, will he be content to eat, drink and be merry
for tomorrow he will die.   Nor will he be satisfied with rosebuds.   But is it not, in all truth, conceivable that the epoch
upon which we are about to enter may be neither reactionary
nor revolutionary but one in which the present—and a more
intense appreciation and acceptance of it—may be called in to
redress the balance of the future and the past?   The wine, as
Coryat said, is always on the table.   Because we learn not to
despise it, there is no need to get drunk.

IV. THE LIBERTY OF SELF-RENEWAL

FOREWORD

THE ROMANTIC IDEA

ROMANTICISM IN ART

ROMANTICISM AND SOCIETY

MARITAIN'S CLASSICAL METHOD

MARITAIN ON EQUALITY

CONCLUSION

FOREWORD

A DIVISION between those who think classically and those who think romantically has long been recognized. The terms are vague and not mutually exclusive, but there are no others in which to describe a conflict of which, in the spheres of politics, of art and of morals, we are all aware. Some of us are happy in feeling that our allegiance is divided: we may be romantics in our distrust of authoritarianism in politics or of a too rigid orthodoxy in manners, and at the same time classicists in our dislike of vagueness, in our care for lucidity and the rule of law, and in our preferring the forms of verse to *vers libre*. Nevertheless, the division is real and has been the occasion of ferocious controversy.

If it be true, as I think it is, that the integrity of the human personality—the power of each man, as an integrated being, to exercise moral choice—is now threatened by collective materialism using physical science as its weapon, it becomes true that classicists and romantics, who alike cherish that integrity, may see a common advantage in their ceasing to tear at each other's throats. They are under no obligation to seek uniformity of view; to do so would be to obscure one of the most profound and productive of human distinctions; but they may be newly inclined to recognize, as philosophers and artists, that an evil power has arisen against them both which demands that they put away the harshness of their enmity. Such a healing of wounds may be brought nearer if the reader of this little group of essays is brought to see the ancient conflict between romanticism and classicism, first from the romantic, and afterwards, in the context of Maritain, from the classical point of view.*

* In the pages which immediately follow, I have used *Classicist* to mean not only, as the dictionary says, " an upholder of classic style or form " but one whose habit of mind inclines him, in life and in art, to emphasize the value of authority and order. My distinction between the substantives *Romantic* and *Romanticist* is taken, for convenience, from Mr. Barzun's book, and is explained as it arises.

THE ROMANTIC IDEA

A DISTINGUISHED book by Mr. Jacques Barzun provides a valuable basis of discussion.* The writer is Associate Professor of History at Columbia University. He is what is sometimes called, a little clumsily, a " cultural historian "—a forbidding phrase by which we must not, in this instance, allow ourselves to be forbidden. It means only a historian who likes to consider his subject from the point of view of the human mind as it is expressed by philosophers and artists. This form of historical specialization is as justifiable as any other, but is more perilous than most. Naval history or diplomatic history consists partly of verifiable fact and partly of interpretation. Cultural history is nearly all interpretation. You must not misquote Rousseau or Goethe, nor must you quote them in such a way as to fortify your own prejudice and distort the context. An honest cultural historian will draw attention to authorities which appear to contradict him; he will raise, in order to meet, opposition to his argument; he will put a demonstrative finger through the holes in his own generalizations; but, apart from this, he is dangerously free. Nevertheless, if, like Mr. Barzun, he is honest in these respects, he may be of great value if we go to meet him in the right spirit. The right spirit is not that of a particularizing critic, who, as he turns the pages, writes " Yes " or " No " beside each paragraph to mark his agreements and disagreements. It is, rather, a spirit of meditation. A work of cultural history performs its greatest service and receives its greatest tribute when a reader allows it to rest upon his knee and

* *Romanticism and the Modern Ego.* By JACQUES BARZUN. Boston: Little, Brown and Co. London: Secker and Warburg. 18s.

his mind to move widely and freely over the historian's subject.

Though Mr. Barzun would probably disclaim any such intent, it is true to say that what he discusses is the future of the world. This is a subject which, in its entirety, cannot be discussed, just as a building cannot be seen whole. You may rise in the air and look upon a building in plan, or you may consider it in elevation from any point of the compass, or you may go into it. Each view is a partial view, but each view enables important deductions to be made about the whole building. Mr. Barzun looks at the future from the point of view of the struggle between romanticism and classicism. Which of these two ways of living and thinking will prevail? Is there any alternative to the historical see-saw between them? If he can give a satisfying answer to these questions, he will have taken a view of the future which is admittedly partial, but is nevertheless one which will enable important deductions to be made about the whole.

One of his chapters is headed " Romantic Art ", and another " Romantic Life ". A reader who allows his mind to play freely upon the book finds that the emphasis of his thought moves between these two aspects of the subject. Sometimes, as he allows the volume to rest upon his knee, he finds that he is looking to the future from an artist's point of view and is asking himself such questions as whether, in literature, painting and music, a romantic or a classical revival is in prospect, and, if so, what influence it will have upon society; and sometimes he finds that he is looking to the future from the point of view of man, the political or social animal, and is asking what his way of thought will be, and what demand he will make upon art, and what importance, if any, he will attach to it. The present discussion may be similarly divided. We may, then, speak first of the Romantic Idea itself, of what romanticism is; and consider afterwards the application of the Romantic Idea to art and to society, preserving always a sense of the relationship between them.

At the outset we must be troubled a little by definitions. A formidable and entertaining section of Mr. Barzun's volume is given to a sampling of modern uses of the word " romantic ", from which it emerges that the word has been used to mean almost anything. It has been used by Havelock Ellis, in his introduction to Landor's *Imaginary Conversations*, to mean " formless ":—

·But beyond these limits he is wanting in architectonic power— the power of duly proportioning a great whole—and sprawls about in as purely romantic fashion as Spenser.

Nevertheless Jullien in his *Hector Berlioz* used it in an opposite sense, asking whether it is not " characteristic of romanticism that the form takes precedence over the subject . . ." and these contradictory uses are unending. Mr. Barzun's quotations show that the word is used by respectable writers to mean " unreal " and " realistic ", " conservative " and " revolutionary ", " soulful " and " materialistic ". The confusion has gone so far that no one can hope to establish a usage which will be generally observed, and the best that any writer can do is to define his own terms for the purposes of his own discussion. In order to do this, Mr. Barzun makes a useful preliminary distinction. He points out that, in English, the word " Romanticism " gives two other words: " romantic " and " romanticist ", and reserves the word " romanticist " for those men who belonged historically to what is ordinarily called the romantic period—to those men, that is to say, who, whatever their differences of idea and method, were born between 1770 and 1815, and " achieved distinction in philosophy, statecraft and the arts during the first half of the nineteenth century ". By speaking of these men as, historically, " romanticists ", the word " romantic " is left free to describe all philosophers, artists and statesmen, of whatever date, who have been spiritual inheritors of the romantic idea or of what Mr. Barzun calls intrinsic romanticism. To make this verbal distinction clears the air a little, but it by no means avoids the babel which attends the use of the word romanticism itself.

What are the permanent elements in human nature which may properly be described as romantic? It is a tendency to confuse the idea itself with particular manifestations or aberrations of it which has enabled the respectable writers quoted by Mr. Barzun so often to contradict themselves and one another. He himself seeks below the particular manifestations for the source from which they sprang.

> What we want [he says] as a definition of intrinsic romanticism is the thing that gave rise to—and that incidentally explains—all the other attitudes I have enumerated. Why did some romanticists attack Reason, why did some turn Catholic, why were some liberal, others reactionary? Why did some praise the Middle Ages and others adore the Greeks? Clearly, the one thing that unifies men in a given age is not their individual philosophies but the dominant problem that these philosophies are designed to solve. In the romantic period . . . this problem was to create a new world on the ruins of the old. The French Revolution and Napoleon had made a clean sweep. Even before the Revolution, which may be taken as an outward show of an inward decay, it was no longer possible to think, act, write, or paint as if old forms had life.

Pausing for a moment to deny unqualified assent to that last, sweeping sentence, we may allow the author to proceed:—

> The critical philosophers of the eighteenth century had destroyed their own dwelling place [he continues]. The next generation must build or perish. Whence we conclude that romanticism is first of all constructive and creative; it is what may be called a solving epoch, as against the *dis*solving eighteenth century.

At this point, let the book rest. Meditate upon it.

A note of alarm has been sounded. Historical writers have sometimes a disconcerting habit of forcing the modern issue. At the least provocation they can become damnably topical— " damnably " because the effort leads them to distort history, or to over-simplify their comment upon past ages, in order to tighten the bond between their historical argument and what their readers will find in tomorrow's newspaper. It is one of Mr. Barzun's qualities that he is generally free from this fault, but at this particular point the reader trembles for him. Tomorrow's newspaper will assuredly say that our task also is " constructive and creative " and that we are upon the threshold of a " solving epoch " which shall succeed the dissolution of our immediate past. Tomorrow's newspaper will say this in the hope of winning the hearts of that increasing number of mankind who would like to believe that revolutions are complete, that you can turn out an epoch as you turn out a room, and that new worlds are new.

None of this is true. Change itself is always the resultant of diverse and enduring conservatisms. The eighteenth century did not dissolve in the sense of disappearing. Its forces shifted their incidence; other forces were added; the direction of the resultant changed; but in Talleyrand and Metternich the " old forms " of statesmanship lived on. What was true of statesmanship was true of art also and of the ordinary ways of society. It will be as true tomorrow morning. Certain epochs are more " constructive " than others; they contribute more new, or seemingly new, forces to the aggregate of the old; but none is " creative ", unless a man may be said to create the bricks which he makes with old straw and piles upon ancient foundations. The point is worth making because to represent the romantic idea itself as being a wind from heaven or nowhere is to play into the hands of the authoritarian detractors of it. Their notion of it is that it is anarchical, sentimental, escapist and chaotic; they wish, therefore, to enslave man and art for his own good. They say that romanticism is morally and æsthetically licentious, and offer, as a saving alternative, the so-called liberties of a new (or an old) order. To dissociate romanticism from its inheritance is to invite this criticism of it and to emphasize, as its enemies do, not its nature but its accidental extravagances.

Although the quoted paragraph at which we paused was momentarily alarming, Mr. Barzun, as he proceeds towards his definition, is careful not to overstate his case. He is so far from claiming that the romantic movement was rootless in the past that he is able to say that " *intrinsic* romanticism, that of the particular individual, is just as alive today as it has ever been, for it is a human constant ". As soon as this ground has been taken up, the discussion acquires a deep significance. It ceases to be an argument between æsthetic cliques, or political parties, or religious sects, and becomes an attempt (which, as will be seen, Maritain and the great classicists also make) to distinguish between the constants and the variables, and to regard the fortunes and aspirations of mankind in the light of that distinction. And if, in recognizing it as a human constant, the discussion does honour to romanticism, it must do equal honour to the forces opposed to it, and recognize them, not by their extravagances, not by their fanatical insistences upon particular sectarian rules, but by their desire to fight the battle of life within the shelter of a formal discipline. This may be called timidity but is, in another aspect, a noble selflessness, and is at any rate a human constant.

Unless we see what is ordinarily called the Romantic-Classical controversy as a struggle between two opposed tendencies of human nature, a veritable expression of man's division against himself, the controversy will remain upon the level of a schoolboys' debate; but if we can approach the problem with real generosity of mind and, while maintaining our own point of view, understand why our opponents are willing to suffer for theirs, the case is altered. The question is not whether Mr. X can assemble a clique of neo-classicists sufficiently powerful to damn the work of Mr. Y by calling it romantic, or whether either group of artists can affiliate itself to some political group from which flow power and purges. Artists have nothing to do with power or purges. They are the vision of man, the eyes of his spirit. The deepest crime they can commit is to persecute one another. Each of us is inclined by temperament or training or by both towards a romantic view of art and life or towards a classical view of them; but we miss the point of life itself—that its beauty and variety as well as its suffering spring from its divisions—if we do not recognize the validity *for them* of our opponents' truth.

The issue, then, is not: Which of the two views is right and which wrong, which orthodox and which heretical? It is, rather: Upon which will the emphasis of the future be laid? And from this question arises another: Is it possible that, in preserving this abiding controversy, which socially, æsthetically and morally has so tormented the world, men have at last suffered enough, so that they will seek and find a way to transcend it? This in itself may be regarded by neo-classicists as a " romantic " idea. Some, the materialists, will condemn it for that reason, saying, in their old-fashioned way, that man, being an economic animal, is incapable of transcendence and that life is, in its very nature, an economic war. But those neo-classicists whom Mr. Barzun calls the neo-Thomists and whom (I believe mistakenly) he treats as hostile will not necessarily set their faces against a reconciliation between the authority to which they refer and the romantic idea. They will oppose it if romanticism is considered by them to be, or aggressively represents itself as being, godless, unfaithful and licentious, but that is its enemies' picture of it —a picture that the neo-Thomists, if such men as Maritain are to be reckoned among them, are scholarly and gentle enough to reject.

There are passages in Mr. Barzun's book which will put up the bristles of those to whom the word romanticism is a menace and an offence, but they will not blind men who rightly care for the disciplines of style to the justice of his definitions or to the opportunity they give for reconciliation between philosophers and artists who, though separated in dogma, have in common that they are men of the spirit.   For him, if we may be allowed to compress and paraphrase, romanticism is a passion to renew life, springing from an awareness of the contrast between man's greatness and wretchedness, his power and his weakness, his opportunity and his plight, and fortified by a philosophy which transcends and harmonizes this felt disharmony.   The stumbling-block here is in the indefinite article—" a philosophy ", and it is right to add that Mr. Barzun's own phrase is: " a philosophy, a religion, a faith ". Pascal, he adds, " found this faith in ascetic Christianity ", whereas the romanticists found it " in many different objects of belief—pantheism, Catholicism, socialism, vitalism, art, science, the national state ".   There are men who, reading this, will slam the door in romanticism's face.   They are pledged; they recognize only one legitimate " object of belief ", not a dozen; romanticism threatens them with dangerous bedfellows.   So it does; so does life; both are dangerous.   But romanticism, like life, is not itself a religion but one of the ways in which religion may be expressed.   It is an instrument of the spirit that may be used or abused.

ROMANTICISM IN ART

A GREAT part of the opposition to romanticism, where it is not merely confused or bitterly partisan, arises among religious men who feel that a form of artistic expression cannot be for them which so easily reflects philosophies or religions other than their own. As dogmatists they are suspicious of romanticism because it is inclusive. Sometimes, even as Christians, they are on their guard against it because it may leave room for the lion to lie down, or to rise up, with the lamb.

Against this suspicion, romanticism is not to be defended by any form of denial. It is not the doctrine of an excluding sect; pagans and Christians alike may be romantics; but it has certain distinguishing characteristics of which the first is that romanticism is concerned always with the nature and essence of the things it treats of rather than with their appearances, and with their appearances only in so far as they indicate nature and essence. For this reason, it is often accused of being unreal or, in recent jargon, " escapist ", by those whose interest is primarily in appearances, whereas, in truth, what it seeks, or " escapes " to, is a reality more profound than they dream of. This is consistent with the definition already given. The search for the reality underlying appearances is part of a search for something that will " transcend and harmonize a felt disharmony ".

To this search, anti-romantic materialists are necessarily opposed. They also observe the disharmony. They notice that, amid the abundance of nature, man is hungry or that, with the delights of peace always before him, he is at war, and they say: this disharmony is contrary to his material interest; if, in our art, we represent it in its true appearances, man will see how his interest suffers, how much richer or less belligerent he might be, and will apply interested remedies. This is the philosophical justification of naturalism. It always fails, and fails for two reasons: first that man, being in his flesh emotional and in his essence a spirit, is not ultimately amenable to materialistic self-interest; and, secondly, that naturalism is barren in the sense in which statistics, however interesting in themselves, are barren—the reader's imagination is not impregnated; he is not enabled to imagine for himself what lies outside his immediate experience or the immediate experience transferred to him by the naturalistic author or statistician.

The anti-romantic materialists make one of two replies. Either they say that there is nothing " outside " for man to imagine and no harmonizing transcendence to which he may attain, in which case the romantic quest is all moonshine and delusion; or they say—and this reply is relatively new—that they have discovered their own mysticism, their own harmonizing transcendence, and that it consists in the idea of the collectivism of man. The first reply bred naturalism; the answer to it is that which Blake might have made to Zola. The second reply is remarkably interesting and illuminating because, though made by materialists who never tire of attacking romanticism, it is itself romantic, and explains what might otherwise seem inexplicable—the attachment of the collectivists to the symbolists, to Valéry, to Mallarmé, even to Baudelaire, who inherited directly from the romanticists of the first half of the nineteenth century. And because romanticism, as has been said, is not an excluding sect, we, if we happen to be individualists and of a liberal mind, ought not to set our faces against the romanticism of men who happen to be collectivists, any more than a Christian romantic should refuse to acknowledge his fellowship with a pagan romantic. Whether a collectivist persists in what we consider his collective error is no æsthetic concern of ours and ought not to affect our æsthetic criticism. We are concerned, as artists and critics, to distinguish between artists, not to persecute men whose religion or policy differs from our own.

We may return, then, perhaps with a new collectivist recruit, to that distinguishing characteristic of romanticism which Mr. Barzun expresses when he says that "romanticism *is* realism". His exposition of this truth, which many will at first consider paradoxical, is to be quoted at length. After saying what is almost true—that the neo-classicism of the eighteenth century perished from an excess of abstraction and "generality", he proceeds to show what the romanticists aimed at and accomplished and how they renewed the life of art:

As against poetic diction and "noble" words, the romanticists admitted all words, especially the neglected host of common words; as against the exclusive use of a selected Græco-Roman mythology, they took in the Celtic and Germanic; as against the uniform setting and tone of classical tragedy, they studied and reproduced the real diversities known as "local colour". As against the antique subjects and the set scale of pictorial merits prescribed by the Academy, they took in the whole world, seen and unseen, and the whole range of colours. As against the academic rules prohibiting the use of certain chords, tonalities and modulations, they sought to use and give shape to all manageable combinations of sound.

They rediscovered the Middle Ages and by extending the interest of art " to remote places such as America and the Near East, earned the name of ' exotic ' for their pains ". They drew the subjects of their art from every class and condition of men. And finally—

As against the materialistic view that whatever is must be tangible, they made room in their notion of reality for the world of dreams, the mysterious in man and in nature, and the supernatural. All this they did deliberately, with the patience and tenacity of pioneers and explorers.

Now, what we are entitled to do as we read this is to mark the similarities between their case and our own, as long as we mark the dissimilarities as well.

The similarities are plain. After nineteenth-century literature had reached and passed its zenith, there was a magnificent after-glow. Hardy in prose, Yeats in poetry, to name but two names, handed on the romantic tradition, which by the Georgians was re-tested and renewed. The war of 1914 snapped the thread. A fierce materialistic reaction set in. All writers who " made room in their notion of reality for the mysterious in man and in nature ", or sought a reality within appearances, or struggled to discover in their art a philosophy that should harmonize the felt disharmony between man's opportunity and his plight—all romantic writers, that is to say, except a few, like Yeats himself, who were too dangerous to attack or threw meat to the wolves—were pursued and denounced. The result by 1922 was expressed by Hardy in a passage which I have quoted before:

The thoughts of any man of letters concerned to keep poetry alive cannot but run uncomfortably on the precarious prospects of English verse at the present day. . . . And a forward conjecture scarcely permits the hope of a better time unless men's tendencies should change. . . . Whether owing to the barbarizing of taste in the younger minds by the dark madness of the late war . . . or from any other cause, we seem threatened with a new Dark Age.

The Dark Age endured. Its leading characteristics may be described, with only superficial changes, in the terms used by Mr. Barzun to describe the conditions of art against which the romanticists rebelled. In the Twenties and Thirties of this century, poetic diction and " noble " words were not required; on the contrary, they were proscribed; but the result was the same as it had been at the end of the *ancien régime*—an artificial and dandyish restriction of the vocabulary. In our Twenties and Thirties there was an exclusive use of collectivist mythology; a uniform setting and tone of modernistic plaintiveness —as rigid in its formlessness as ever classical tragedy had been in its forms; there was an insistence upon " contemporary " subjects as pedantic as the classicists' insistence on the " antique ", and, in all the arts, a " set scale of merits " laid down, not by the Academy but by the coteries. The rules were so narrow and so strict that the writings of those who obeyed them gradually became incomprehensible by all but a few initiates.

Upon these conditions another war descended; the coteries dissolved in stifled silence; and it would seem that if, in the future, the life of art is to be renewed, the renewal must come from artists who are prepared to admit all words, to use all mythologies, to admit the whole range of colours, and to " take in the whole world, seen and unseen ". Whether they will call themselves Romantics matters not at all. Whether the timorous call them " escapist " or " exotic " will matter even less. Nothing matters except that they study and reproduce the " real diversities " of experience—that is to say that they be romantic realists in spirit, if not in name, and seek that harmonizing beauty which is the essence of all things.

This they will not achieve—indeed, in the present condition of the world, they will achieve nothing worth achieving—if they, in their turn, organize themselves as an exclusive and self-advertising sect. It may be thought that an embroidered waistcoat and another battle of *Hernani* would do no harm, but the battle that the romantic realists have to fight is not with other artists, not even with the coteries of Hardy's Dark Age, but a battle—the last of western civilization if it is not won—against what, though the phrase is violent, I dare to call the gangsters of the spirit. There is a gangsterism of art as there is of politics. The purpose of each is to discredit, disintegrate and enslave the human personality—to drive men into the belief that they have no real existence except as units in a mass, to deafen them to the disharmony between their opportunity and their plight, and to deaden in them the hope of salvation. There have been tyrants enough in the past, but never before in the world's history has there been a cult of gangsterism such as there is today, a cult tacitly subscribed to by many who are unconscious of its existence. One of its methods is the debasement of art, the mechanization of it, the reducing of it to the condition of a mass-product, for, if man should learn to regard art as a thing not pertaining to beauty and truth but only to opinion, then he will lose his vision, and become what the gangsters would have him be—an animal, herded.

The stakes for which we have to play are so high that we may well ask whether a time has not come in which romantics and classicists, being men of the spirit and not gangsters, ought not to sink or, rather, to transcend their differences. On the side of romanticism, the opposition is, in the main, defensive. For a quarter of a century " romantic " has been used as a term of abuse, and abuse begets defence. Mr. Barzun sometimes uses the tone of partisanship in speaking of classicists, but we need not imitate him in this. In any case, if we remember that a part of his harshness springs from his having emotionally identified them with Louis Quatorze and from his dislike of that monarch, what he writes is valuable as description and analysis. The human mind, he says, desires unity within the human breast and in the institutions sheltering man.

Now the straightest path to unity is to choose from all the possible ways of living those that seem to the ruling powers most profitable, most sensible, most general; and to enforce these as a code for public and private behaviour. . . . Such a system produces stability in the state and with it all the attributes of the static: fixed grandeur, dignity, authority, and high polish, while in the individual it produces morality and peace. . . . This, I take it, is the view of life properly called " classic ", irrespective of whether it was enforced upon Europe under Louis XIV, or is advocated at Chicago by the classic-minded neo-Thomists.

These are the classicists as Mr. Barzun sees them. From the classical point of view, he says:—

... everything the romanticist thinks and does is wrong: far from taking the short cut to unity and peace, he insists upon the reality of double-mindedness and self-contradiction. He rejects the simple conventions that bind men together and prefers human diversity. Sharply aware of his own desires, he argues that the social rule is oppressive and unjust, so that he becomes, potentially at least, a public anarchist. ... He is therefore in the position of constantly bewailing a condition for which he is solely to blame. And the last consolation is denied him, for having refused all help from social conventions, his art, philosophy and religion are bound to remain diversified, many-shaped, chaotic—hence unsatisfying.

It is true that there are classicists or, as we should have preferred to say, authoritarians who have brought such an attack upon themselves. They have distorted the romantic idea and have even gone to the absurd length of identifying it, because Hitler was emotional, with Hitlerism, and, because Communism was revolutionary, with Communism. Some, in their hatred and fear of romanticism, have allied themselves with the materialists in bitter criticism of it. Nevertheless, in the sphere of art, reconciliation between the two points of view is not impossible. Certainly, it is necessary and urgent.

Reconciliation is not impossible now, as it was a few years ago, because the wound inflicted on the world by the collective materialists is deeper than men's former prejudices. Mr. Barzun's failure to recognize this is the principal weakness of his book. As long as his argument is purely critical, the defect does not appear A chapter in which he shows how grossly and ignorantly Rousseau has been misrepresented by the enemies of romanticism is, for example, vigorous and unanswerable. But when he gives a topical twist to his historical discourse, he often leaves an impression of his being out of touch with contemporary Europe. Those whom he calls " the classic-minded neo-Thomists " are less afraid of romanticism than they were, and the romantics are less afraid of them. There is a fear recognizably greater than either of these internecine fears. A charity of common suffering and an energy of common endurance have entered even into criticism.

The classicists, though they approach the transcendent harmony by the way of disciplines which romantic realists do not accept as necessary, are not, except for the purposes of dying controversy, fools; the neo-Thomists are authoritarians, but not materialistic authoritarians, not gangsters. This romantic realists understand. Correspondingly, the classicists themselves, perceiving that the real threat to what they love and honour is not the romantics' liberal diversity but a freezing of the whole world into the forms of a godless materialism, are less disposed than they were to speak of romanticism as if it were synonymous with chaos. Nor is the romantic realism of the future likely to be open to such a suspicion. It is not without reason that the possibility of a classical revival is so often spoken of in the same breath with the possibility of a romantic revival. Romanticism is accepting new disciplines, and classicism a new liberty. This double acceptance, a combining of strength against materialism, must give its character to the art of the future if art is to be again what at its greatest it has always been—a sword against pride, vainglory and hypocrisy, and hardness of heart.

ROMANTICISM AND SOCIETY

A RECONCILIATION between romantic and classical artists must, if it is to be effective, be part of a wider reconciliation between romanticism and classicism as social principles, and if we are to consider whether this wider reconciliation is possible, we have to ask first what romanticism is in the context of society and what is the nature of the classical opposition to it. Again Mr. Barzun's book will be continually of value. What has already emerged from it is the helpfulness of the author's refusal to define romanticism by its accidental products—emotion or liberty or what you will—and of his determination to seek its historical causes and its governing purpose. From this determination arose one prevailing word: harmony. Romanticism was defined as a passion to renew life, springing from an awareness of the contrast between man's greatness and his wretchedness, and fortified by a philosophy which transcends and harmonizes this " felt disharmony ". This definition is as valid socially as it is æsthetically, and it is legitimate to ask whether it is not true also that the classical principle is, in essence, harmonious, though the classical harmony is sought for by a means different from the romantic. May not this be the grounds of a reconciliation too long postponed? This is the conclusion which we seem now to be approaching, but it has not yet been reached, and the best way of approach will be to attempt a restatement of the romantic principle as it affects the relationship of the individual to society, to subject that restatement to what Mr. Barzun calls " the classical opposition ", and to discover whether, in the modern world, that opposition is still irreconcilable.

To clear the ground, and at the risk of over-compression, it is necessary to say briefly what is meant here by the phrase: " classical opposition ". The classicism to be spoken of now is that which, under the influence of Malherbe, sprang up in France as an answer to a preceding disorder in life and art, which ushered in the Age of Reason, which broke down (or seemed to break down) with the passing of the *ancien régime*, but has, in fact, never perished, and has among its representatives today not only those whom Mr. Barzun calls the neo-Thomists of Chicago but a multitude of other humane and scholarly men who, whether or not they base their philosophy on Aquinas, look for a freedom arising from order rather than for an order distilled from various freedoms. They set a higher value upon authority than romantics set upon it, but they are not tyrants unless fear makes tyrants of them. They are not advocates of a frozen and " static " society. Their view is this: let man, they say, who is weak and fallible, limit the area of his decision by certain acceptances; let him find peace by circumscribing the area of his personal fallibility; in art, let him recognize, as the romantic Wordsworth did, the liberty and strength accorded to him by the formal discipline of the sonnet; in religion, politics and the conduct of his personal life, let him make corresponding recognitions.

The holding of this view may lead to abuses and extravagances, to pedantry, censoriousness and obscurantism. It may, even, tempt cowardly minds into association with collective materialists or totalitarians who so pervert the doctrine of acceptance and authority that they say: render unto Cæsar the things that are God's. But this is not classicism; it is a perversion of it, just as anarchy is not romanticism but a perversion of it. Classicism itself, as we strive to understand it, is based, not in matters of faith only but in all else, on the phrase: " whose service is perfect freedom ". Are romantics, whose emphasis is on the last word, enemies of men whose emphasis lies farther back?

The historical romanticists owed much to Rousseau's doctrine of the General Will, and, particularly in France, this doctrine has had a continuing influence upon the practice of democratic government. The classicists, therefore, use Rousseau as a stick with which to beat romanticism. If he was evil or at best fallacious, they argue, then romanticism is evil and fallacious. Look at Vichy, they cry, and see what tyranny has resulted from French democratic decay, to which the romantics as hastily answer that Vichy was an example of that authoritarianism which the classicists love. Here is a deadlock of debate, and, if collective materialism is not to flourish upon our divisions, a way out of it must be found.

The deadlock arises from an error committed by both parties to the argument—that of basing their attack upon the distortions, and not upon the inmost truth, of their opponents' teaching. Even the great Maritain interprets Rousseau too harshly. In his *Principes d'une Politique Humaniste* he speaks of the idea of the *volonté générale* as a " myth "; and says that " *la démocratie conçue à la manière de Rousseau supprime l'autorité* [by which he means authority with a genuine moral foundation] *et garde le pouvoir* ". To this democracy he gives the name: *Démocratie anarchiste-masquée*, a name which expresses in epitome the classicists' case against Rousseauism, against the " *démocratie libérale ou bourgeoise* " of the nineteenth century, and against romanticism itself. But here there is a confusion of ideas. The defects of nineteenth-century democracy sprang, not from the doctrine of the General Will but from a steadily increasing corruption of it. Rousseau's idea of the General Will was of something altogether different from—and was, indeed, a designed corrective to—the Wish of the Majority for the Time Being. Mr. Barzun performs a valuable service in

insisting upon this distinction.   He goes so far as to say that,
for Rousseau, the General Will " is equivalent to the good of
the state "—a proposition which presents so broad a target
that he would be a bold philosopher who undertook to defend
it against Maritain's rapier; and I would rather say that, by
Rousseau, the General Will was thought of as being the will
of what we should now call the Continuing People—not of
today's majority but of men present and men future; not even
of them considered as a mass marching through some theo-
retical polling-booth but of them considered as individuals.
The General Will was, for Rousseau, a mystical resultant of
all individual wills.   The business of government was to
interpret its deferred wisdom, and thereby to extract a harmony resting upon the integrity of the individual soul, and
upon *its* authority, from the " felt disharmony " of a grouped
majority and a grouped minority.

The real trouble with the General Will is that it cannot,
in political practice, be ascertained.   Mr. Barzun rightly says
that " the test of it is pragmatic, it appears in the sequel ".
The result has been that an impatient world has tended more
and more to confuse it with the Wish of the Majority for the
Time Being.   In countries, of which France is a leading example, whose constitutions have been unbalanced in the sense
that they have provided too little check upon the arbitrary
rule of that Wish, the consequences have been unfortunate;
but in other countries, such as England, where, until lately,
Executive and Legislature have been more shrewdly balanced,
there has been less scope for the perversions of Rousseauism.
In England, moreover, the blessed and saving condition of
there being a non-elective judiciary has enabled the expression
of what may well be spoken of as the deferred wisdom of the
Continuing People.   The Law, as it is understood and ad-
ministered among us, is not an impulse of the present majority.
Though it rests upon a different theory, its effects are closely

analogous to the effect that might have been produced by a genuine application of Rousseau's teaching, and it is so far recognized by us as an expression of the general will that each of us, in obeying it, feels that he is obeying himself.

This conception of the individual obedient to himself was a leading idea of Rousseau's. The classicists say that it is equivalent to the idea of anarchy, and there are to this day romantics who so pervert it; but, if rightly understood, it proceeds not to anarchy but to justice, a known, continuing and compassionate justice resting upon a profound moral authority. It is a part of that harmony, transcending the " felt disharmony " of opinions in conflict, which is sought for by romantics and classicists alike; the difference between the two schools of thought being that whereas classicists, who wish to discover an obedience which is freedom, acknowledge an authority external to themselves, romantics, engaged in the same quest, look for authority within themselves. To this a classicist might answer: " My authority is of heaven, yours of earth," but this antithesis is false. His ultimate authority is shown to him by his faith in God; a romantic's is shown to him by his faith in that variety of human experience, that integrity of the human person, through which, he believes, divinity is expressed on earth. Between such men the difference is not irreconcilable.

In each succeeding age, the romantic idea has to be differently applied and is open to new perversions. In the age upon the threshold of which we now stand, it will be forced into alliance with classicism by the brutal challenge of collective materialism, which is an equal threat to the moral authority of the classicists and to the romantic conception of variety and integrity. It would seem to follow that, in the days to come, romanticism will tend more and more to dissociate itself from Rousseauism, precisely because collective materialism has perverted it and laid it open to such strictures as Maritain's.

The romantic idea is not anarchical nor is it materialistic. In both these directions it has been perverted and misconceived.

Romanticism, in its application to society, rests upon the assumption that neither the state nor any other organization of man has a mystical reality. The state is a practical convenience, not to be worshipped. The individual, under whatever gods may be for him, is sovereign within himself, but has delegated to the state certain powers over him. These powers—and here is the essential distinction between the romantic and the totalitarian ideas—do not extend to the whole area of his life. Certain rights of the individual are reserved by him from government by the community, as in America state-rights are reserved from the Federal Government. But within the area of power ceded to it the state coerces the individual and is entitled to his loyalty.

A good state, in the romantic view, not only abstains from coercion outside the area proper to it, but, even within that area, coerces as little as possible and gives the greatest possible scope to individualism. Thus, although in times of public danger it may compel a man to military service, it will mitigate the burden of conscription by allowing him, so far as possible, to choose the form of his service, at sea or by land or in the air, and will encourage him by every means in its power to preserve his individuality within the bonds of discipline. Again, in the romantic view, the state ought not to be guided only by what the Rulers-for-the-Time-Being consider to be the common good. They are fallible; they should recognize that a perpetual balance to their errors is to be found in individualistic self-development. Therefore, uniformity is not good in itself, but is to be thought of always as being bad until it has been proved to be inevitable.

This, which is true for romantics in matters of conduct and appearance, is doubly true in matters of thought and faith. As they do not wish women to dress uniformly and so are advocates sometimes of charming or ridiculous extravagances of costume, so they do not wish men to think uniformly and are guilty sometimes of a wild extravagance of doctrine. This often brings them into conflict with the classicists, whose view of discipline and dogma leads them to consider the romantic love of variety as dangerously heretical. It is necessary to understand that this love of variety is not in its nature rebellious, but arises from the romantic belief that through variety alone are balance and harmony attainable.

As the good state must honour the human person even within the state's legitimate area of power, so, the romantics argue, a state is necessarily bad which invades the area of the individual's reserved and undelegated sovereignty. The state may, in certain circumstances, compel a man to abstain from actions or, even, compel him to act, but it must not compel or induce him to think. Mr. Kerrison Preston, in a recent book on *Blake and Rossetti*, called attention to a saying of Blake's which might stand as a warning on the desk of every teacher wise enough to receive it :—

He told Crabb Robinson : " There is no use in education. I hold it wrong. It is the great sin. It is eating of the tree of the knowledge of good and evil. . . . There is nothing in all that. Everything is good in God's eyes."

This is an extreme statement of the romantic view. Less extremely, it may be said that propaganda, or whatever produces the uniformity and subjection of the human mind, " is the great sin "—a sin which is the greater if it is committed by artists. Their duty is to uncongeal the blood of the human imagination, to revive its sluggish pulse—in brief, to enable men to imagine for themselves ever more widely, more intensely and more compassionately. The duty of an educationist is, correspondingly, not to think for men but to enable them to think for themselves.

This does not mean that a romantic refuses to recognize

that there are such things as conventions and acceptances which enable freedom. It lies, indeed, at the root of his faith to recognize the validity, for them, of other men's conventions. He does not fight against them, but he does fight against the imposition of them by force or fraud upon those whose liberty is not enabled but restricted by them. Now it happens that whereas in the past classicists were sometimes inclined, in a perversion of classicism, to be inquisitorial in defence of what they believed to be truth, and romantics were inclined, in a perversion of romanticism, to be intolerant of all rules, whether of morals, of art or of law, and so brought upon themselves the reproof of anarchy, all this today is changed. The romantic view is remote from anarchy, the classical view from intolerance. The two accursed words, taken together, describe, the first in terms of the spirit, the second in terms of the flesh, that collective materialism or gangsterism against which romantics and classicists are now jointly concerned to defend the whole life of the spirit.

MARITAIN'S CLASSICAL METHOD *

THE mind of Jacques Maritain has two supreme virtues: first, that it glows with charities and is marvellously exempt from spiritual pride; secondly, that, in all the years which have passed since his first critical studies of Bergson appeared in Paris, it has never allowed him, in any of his work, to play down to an audience. On the one hand, all that he writes is written in a love of mankind, sprung from his sense of human unity; on the other, he has never suggested, with a view of popularizing his philosophy or using it as an instrument of propaganda, that a philosopher is a kind of witch-doctor who, if we will but listen to him for ten minutes on the wireless, will save us the exercises of faith and reason by telling us for whom we should vote, in what cause we should agitate, and, in brief, precisely what we should do. " I must know ", he says in this volume of essays, " where I am and who I am, before knowing, and in order to know, what I should do," and there could not be a wiser or a gentler answer to those who are inclined to think that philosophy, unless it be debased to a series of rules for conduct, does not concern them.

There are many thousands of students who now go to colleges asking only that they may be taught how to do something—how to farm or how to write shorthand. The response to their demand is called vocational education. If we give it a less pretentious name and call it instead " apprenticeship ", we shall not despise it; for assuredly there is great virtue in apprenticeship to a craft if it be honoured as what it is and not puffed up as what it is not. Nevertheless, to ask: how

* *Redeeming the Time*. By JACQUES MARITAIN. Translated by HARRY LORIN BINSSE. Geoffrey Bles. 12s. 6d.

shall I do this or that? is evidently not a final question. Underlying it is the question: what should I do? And underlying this are the questions: where am I? and: who am I? If the saying of Maritain which has just been quoted were put before students about to choose their courses of study, and before educationists about to prescribe courses, and before legislators about to reform education, they might all be led to ask themselves salutary questions now seldom asked, and the schools of philosophy might be fuller than they are. For philosophy is not removed from common life except in the sense in which it may be said that the heart is removed from the surfaces of the body, and it is Maritain's strength that, though he never pretends to write easily or superficially, he does reward a reader's care with a sense of penetration, of approach to the heart of experience, of struggling towards a truth not of logic only but of life itself.

So important does it seem to be that a mind of the quality of Maritain's should be brought to bear on the contemporary world that it is by no means foolish to urge his book upon readers who might be inclined to shun it on the ground that they lack the philosophical equipment necessary to a full understanding of it. Maritain, it must be admitted, assumes much—for example, in his criticism of Bergson, a knowledge of the teaching of St. Thomas Aquinas not common in Protestant England; and a reader unversed in scholasticism must be prepared to find many words, such as " idealism " and " realism ", used in specialized senses. But this ought not to deter those of us who, though neither Catholics nor theologians, are yet not lazy in our thought. Words are not used in a specialized sense without clear indication that they are being so used, and even those essays which, at first glance, might appear to be exclusively Catholic—for example, " Who is My Neighbour ? " in which the author examines the Catholic doctrine concerning the status of non-Catholics before God—

are found to turn always upon some universal question. What Maritain is asking in " Who is My Neighbour? " is whether the diversity of religious creeds is an insurmountable obstacle to human co-operation. So it always is with him. No flower he touches is for his button-hole. It looks to heaven, has its roots on earth, and is interesting to him, and so to us, because it is not a decoration of his intellect but a part of universal nature. His diverse essays, he justly claims, have one subject: " man in his cultural life and in the complex patterns of his earthly destiny ". There are so-called philosophers in whom so embracing a claim would be a prelude to vagueness or to propaganda. Maritain is never vague, and what he cares for is not that we should act by his instruction, but that, instead of thinking brutally or clumsily or loosely, we should make those clear distinctions and, if possible, those reconciliations which are a way towards truth. In this he is a true Thomist. The work of Aquinas's life was to show that faith was reconcilable with reason, Christianity with Aristotelianism. His critics have said that he thereby limited the scope of reason, for the results of his inquiry were already prescribed before his inquiry began; and some may be inclined to make a corresponding criticism of Maritain. But it is not a criticism which a non-Catholic, who is also a philosopher, ought to make unless he is purely empirical or believes that reason unsupplemented can embrace all available truth. A reader who holds such a view will certainly be so far out of sympathy with Maritain as to be, perhaps, incapable of learning from him, but the rest of us, without necessarily ourselves accepting the authority which he accepts, may perceive that for him it is not an enslavement but a liberation. His acceptance of it is continuously voluntary, because in him reason and revealed truth are in a state of continuously developing reconciliation.

This gives their character, their spiritual style, to all the essays in the present volume.   The first of these, on " Human Equality ", which investigates a subject today urgently controversial, must be considered separately in the pages which follow so that it may be treated with the care it deserves.   Even when this reservation has been made those that remain cannot be analysed one by one; nor can any generalization be made concerning them which would not be lacking in respect for their fullness and the closeness of their argument.   It will be best to attempt no more than to indicate their subjects and to draw from them an idea of the author's method and of the direction of his thought.

" The Political Ideas of Pascal " is an examination of the false position into which Pascal was led by his " illusory notion of a justice among men which, of itself, should have the same universal application as the propositions of Euclid ".   For Maritain, true justice descends from divine reason and requires that human laws vary according to country and to period, and that customs have the force of law; but here, as elsewhere, his criticism, however severe against Pascal's empirical pessimism, is not purely destructive even in its approach to Pascal's errors, for Pascal's concept of custom leads beyond embittered conservatism to " those vital improvements in the spiritual powers of the soul called *habitus*, and form dispositions ", of which the most important are the virtues.   Having gone so far in purely philosophical criticism, destructive and constructive; having, as it were, cleared the ground and established in it the foundations of his own thought, Maritain proceeds with his invariable work of spiritual and practical architecture—practical because spiritual:—

By reflecting [he says] along these lines on the principles of Pascal, we understand—to come back to the central problem of political philosophy offered by the last two centuries—under what concrete conditions [he is thinking, above all, of the education of the masses, not only by instruction that enriches the intellect, but by the drawing out of their virtues]—under what concrete conditions it is proper to summon all human persons who are members of a state to participate, in differing degrees, in its political life.

And though, before the essay is done, the author cannot resist another blow at the Jansenists, his conclusion is liberally, and at the same time precisely, Christian, and contains a warning against the evil of imposing religious domination by external and political means.

This relating of philosophy to common experience, this implicit claim that the parts of common experience by the multiplicity of which mankind is confused cannot be related or harmonized except in a philosophy that has a divine source, is typical of his method.   It informs his treatment of " The Mystery of Israel " and his remarkably open discussion of " The Catholic Church and Social Progress "—open in the sense that what " he proposes regarding Catholicism can be applied, *mutatis mutandis*, to the other Christian bodies ". The same method is applied, though here necessarily at a remove, to an elaborate study of " The Natural Mystical Experience ", which examines not only the kinds of that experience but the ways of approach to it, and is in its turn related to an essay, in many respects the most deeply original in the book, on " Sign and Symbol ".   Maritain shows where lies his disagreement with those who regard religion, metaphysics, mystical experience and poetry as varying metamorphoses of ancient magic, directly opposed, like magic itself, to the line of science and truth; and with those who, while believing magic to be the reverse of science, consider magic and religion to have a common origin, " starting from which they have developed in opposite directions, magic in the direction of illusion, of myth-making and of laziness, religion (dynamic religion) in the direction of heroism and of truth ".

To my mind [says Maritain] our physico-mathematical science is only one of the possible forms of science and one of the degrees of knowledge, knowledge which at its high point is called metaphysics, and, higher still, theology and mystical knowledge. Moreover, both science and metaphysics, like religion and mysticism, and like poetry—each of them in its own fashion a function of the truth— are created to grow up together, and, if man will expend on them the necessary pains and effort, to blossom forth in harmony. . . . Thus all human thought, with its great and at first undifferentiated primordial ramifications, passes, I believe, through a diversity of conditions, or of states of existence and practice. As it is progressively diversified, human thought passes from the condition of magic to the condition of logic.

This power of synthesis, at once bold and serene, this rare gift of projecting his intuitive perception of a single and unifying truth into diverse experiences, constitutes what has been called Maritain's " spiritual style ".

The consequence is that one receives from his work an unfailing impression of harmony, and understands at once that when he says of Bergson, whose genius he profoundly admired, that there was " a kind of Manichæan cleavage " in his view of man as " caught between being something *social*, infra-rational, and something *mystical*, supra-rational ", he is not splitting hairs or scoring a point in Thomist controversy or narrowly insisting upon the orthodoxy of Thomist thought, but is feeling, as well as asserting, a failure, a disharmony, in this part of Bergson's philosophy. " Only reason ", he says —and Aquinas himself would scarcely have phrased it differently :—

Only reason, which is the principle of a moral universe distinct at once from social obedience and mystical impulse, can recognize, in dependence on the laws proper to that universe, the internal hierarchy which subordinates the social entity to the mystical, and at the same time reconciles them with each other. But to posit that subordination and that reconciliation is to get away from Bergsonism.

This is part of a profound examination of " The Two Sources of Morality and Religion ", in which Bergson's theme was the distinction and opposition between that which in moral life proceeds from pressure—from that law of fear imposed by the individual's membership of a group—and that which proceeds from attraction, from " the call of superior souls who commune with the *élan* of the spirit ".   Corresponding with the law of pressure and the law of attraction are two quite separate forms of morality: the closed morality of " social conformism " and the open morality of holiness; and there are, according to Bergson, corresponding with these two moralities, two forms of religion: static religion which develops a myth-making function as a defence against the dissolving power of the intelligence, and dynamic religion, " which is above all a vocation to the mystical life ".   Maritain inevitably feels that these Bergsonian ideas of morals and religion, viewed in the " perspective of doctrinal construction, of philosophy as a system . . . call for serious reservations in spite of the great truths on which they cast light," and it is possible for a non-Catholic reader to feel that while Maritain is demonstrating, in this connexion, Bergson's " doctrinal deficiencies ", he is using the lesser rather than the greater weapons of scholasticism and is narrowing the argument. Criticism, it seems for a moment, is recoiling upon its own prejudices rather than extending itself in interpretation of its subject.

But this is never true of Maritain, and soon he proves it to be untrue in this instance.   When he changes his regard and considers Bergson's *Two Sources* from what he calls the point of view of the spirit and of directive intuitions, he explains that his earlier demonstration of doctrinal delinquencies had, as its purpose, to extend the argument and not, as we had been tempted to suppose, to narrow it.   His object was to show that " philosophy *alone* is not enough in these matters " and he adds this footnote:

Mme. Henri Bergson has made public part of her late husband's will, dated February 8, 1937.   Here are a few sentences from that document. " My reflections have led me closer and closer to Catholicism, in which I see the complete fulfilment of Judaism. I would have become a convert had I not seen in preparation for years the formidable wave of anti-Semitism which is to break upon the world. I wanted to remain among those who tomorrow will be persecuted. But I hope that a Catholic priest will consent, if the Cardinal Archbishop of Paris authorizes it, to come to say prayers at my funeral." A priest did in fact fulfil this wish. Henri Bergson died on January 4, 1941.

Apart from the light that this footnote casts back upon the biography of Bergson, it is valuable as a comment upon, and a justification of, Maritain's critical method. If the event of Bergson's " reflections " had been other than it was, Maritain's examination of their " doctrinal deficiencies " might well have been considered excessive or, at any rate, over-particular, but is seen now to have been deeply relevant to Bergson's philosophical development. If there are any who believe that thought can ever be uncoloured by predilection, or who are so naïve as to suppose that rationalistic materialism, called " scientific ", can be philosophically impartial, they must be allowed, at their own cost, to reject Maritain as what they will call " a Catholic apologist ". Others among us who do not accept the authority of Rome will see, in his acceptance of it, the firm establishment of a point of view, and ask only whether this firmness is *in him* a cause of philosophical steadiness or of distortion. There can be no doubt of the answer. His work is the expression, not of reason alone or of faith alone, or of a compromise between them. It is the expression of an integrated personality, rich, various and profound, which shines from within each subject discussed. Maritain's philosophical approach to the problem of human equality, which has next to be considered, is therefore of the highest interest, and might, if it were understood on a political level, give a new direction to political thought.

THE difficulty is to enable it to be understood on that level. In the first place, its language is not that of the market-place; in the second, we are nowadays little accustomed to think of politics in philosophical terms; in the third, it contains phrases which, if separated from their context, will cause certain men of good will to throw up their hands in horror. For example, the right to the private ownership of material goods is numbered among " the fundamental rights of the human person ". Or, again:

. . . it is an illusion to wish that all may have at the start strictly identical opportunities to mount to the highest degrees in social life.

In their context, these sayings are qualified and supported. Even so, they require of the reader a loyal determination not to be startled by them into supposing that Maritain is saying what he is not, and an equal determination, when Maritain's meaning is clearly understood, not to whittle it away because it is uncomfortable. For, even when qualified, the teachings of this essay are not such as will flatter the victims of demagogues. Its view of equality is flatly opposed to the whole doctrine of equalitarianism. The materialistic catchwords are attacked not from the point of view of an opposed materialism but at their philosophical root. Maritain's central argument implies that many whose advocacy of equalitarianism appears to them as an expression of their Christian good will are utterly deluded, and that Christianity requires of them an altogether different understanding of what equality is. In this sense, the essay is revolutionary. It is not surprising that the author placed it first in his book.

He does not write loosely. To compress his argument is

to be in peril of over-simplification, but, since it cannot be assumed that every reader of this essay has Maritain's book beside him, the risk must be taken if there is to be a basis of discussion.

The idea of equality, he says, is surrounded by geometrical imagery. In applying it to human beings the mind must therefore beware of being misled by this imagery. All lions have a unity of species. If they lived in society and could speak, they would probably insist upon saying that all lions are *equal* in nature, but he will reject such emotional connotations and will take " equality in nature " as being synonymous with unity of nature.

The fact that all men have the same specific nature can be viewed from three points of view: the nominalist, the idealist and the realist. The purely nominalist or empiricist notion of human equality is that the unity in nature between men is unreal and that only the inequalities matter. These inequalities exist; the empiricist's error is not in his recognition of them but in his deeming as nothing the nature or essence that men have in common. He then proceeds to rationalize his error. He attributes, without realizing it, the character and value of specific categories to arbitrary groups; he groups the inequalities, he raises up pseudo-scientific categories of party or caste or race, and shatters, by denying, the unity of the human family. This Maritain calls the anti-Christian philosophy of enslavement. Plainly it is the philosophy of totalitarianism.

The second or " idealist " point of view, which is that of equalitarian philosophers, is next examined. For those who think in this way, the unity of human nature is " the unity of a subsisting Idea, of a Man-in-himself, existing outside time ". Individuals are thus seen as shadows without substance. Equality in species among them is alone considered real. The inequalities among individuals are " pushed aside by the mind " whether they are natural inequalities or social inequalities. An idealist, obsessed by the idea of the Man-in-himself, minimizes natural inequalities or suggests that they are above all the result of artificial social stratifications; and of social inequalities he says that they ought not to exist and that the essential dignity of the Man-in-himself is outraged by them. The idealist error, Maritain says,

lies in the conviction that all human substance reflows within the abstract species alone, and that the reality and value of those individual inequalities . . . are as nothing. But these individual inequalities, despite the burden of sorrow or injustice which the sins of men or the vices of institutions may superimpose on them, are in themselves as necessary for the development and flowering of human life as the diversity of parts for the perfection of a flower or a poem.

This idealist cult of the Man-in-himself, as it rejects natural inequalities, rejects also natural privileges. It requires that they be rigorously levelled; it loathes the very notion of distinction; so that when a professor in an American university chose a number of great men as exemplars of certain periods of civilization, his students were shocked and asked: Why great men? Was it not the mass of men that really mattered? Yet the gifts of nature and natural inequalities exist, and Maritain patiently demonstrates the consequences of an equalitarianism which shuts its eyes to them and will not perceive their value. All the implications of this philosophy are, he says, as incompatible with Christian thought as those of the philosophy of enslavement.

For a statement of Maritain's view of " the realist idea, the true idea of equality ", the reader must go to the philosopher himself. It can be indicated, but not summarized even to the extent that his preliminary attacks on error have here been summarized. The reason is that his constructive argument runs in two main streams which, converging, lead to his conclusion—a stream which may, perhaps, be called the stream of Christian humanism, and another which, deep and powerful though it is, is nevertheless more particular than the first and has its origin in the doctrine of Aquinas. For Maritain's Thomism, expressed with a master's lucidity and a brevity that is irreducible, it is necessary to go to Maritain. Here it can only be urged that no reader be prevented from doing so by any anti-clerical bias in himself. Maritain is a Catholic; it is natural and right that he should show how his faith and his reason, like two streams tributary to a single river, form the current of his final judgement; indeed, it would have been dishonest in him to have done otherwise. Nevertheless, it is by no means necessary to rely upon the authority he quotes—for example, the Encyclical *Summi pontificatus*—in order to reach his conclusion. He himself quotes the Encyclical to " confirm " and " emphasize " an argument which he establishes by philosophical, and not by authoritative, means. It is necessary to say this, and to insist upon it, in order that no one, in the belief that what is offered to him is dependent on an authority which he cannot accept, should neglect Maritain's discourse.

His view may be briefly indicated as follows: The universality of ideas is grounded *in re*. Common humanity is not a mere word; it is ontological and concrete. We are often unaware of it. It often " slumbers in a metaphysical retreat where we can perceive it only as an abstraction ", but in the common experience of misery, in concentration camps, in any common necessity, " man recognizes man "—or, as we should have preferred to say, " men recognize man ". In great joy also and in great love this recognition is made.

If this is true, Maritain continues, if this natural community between men is real, the " orderings and hierarchies which spring and should spring from the very heart of this essential community " are not to be repudiated. Christian realism wishes to develop " fruitful inequalities ", and to interpret the word " equality " not, as equalitarians do, on a plane surface but with the dimension of depth as well. . . . Let us not say that one man is as good as another; that is a nihilistic formula which acquires real meaning only from deep religious pessimism (*vanitas vanitatum, omnis homo mendax*). Let us say that in a man are, *virtualiter*, all men.

Therefore it is an offence against creation " to treat as an *inferior man* a man belonging to some inferior part of the social structure ". An inferiority of condition is not an inferiority of essence, and Christianity, recognizing this, is bound to recognize also that equality of essence is primordial and that social inequalities (which totalitarians and equalitarians raise to a first place in their regard) are secondary. Now social inequalities are of two kinds. Some result from natural inequalities, and it is an offence against nature not to bestow " upon superior persons who are an honour to their own species the same care that men bestow upon their rare plants and their most beautiful stallions "; and some social inequalities are themselves of social origin. These are not, in themselves, wrong. Some, indeed, bear witness to the unconquerable vitality of social life, but they become wrong " if bewildered men wish to erect them into a state of social servitude for the human groups assumed to be inferior ".

Having thus analysed the inequalities, Maritain proceeds to an elaborate definition of social equality itself. First, it is equality in the fundamental rights of the human person: to exist, to preserve one's body, to found a family, to associate, privately to own material goods, " to seek those good things through which a rational creature may perfect himself ", and to seek eternal life in accordance with one's own conscience. Next, it requires equality before the law, and, Maritain adds— quoting Cardinal Verdier, and, for once, leaving definition in the air—" political equality . . . and the making available to all citizens of public employment ". Finally, social equality requires that all should " so far as possible participate ' free of charge ' in the elementary goods needed for human life ".

What Maritain and Cardinal Verdier mean by "political equality" it is hard to understand. Equality of power?—but that is absurd. Equality of status?—but what does that mean other than equality before the law? Let it pass. It is Maritain's only vagueness.

What matters is the conception of Proportional Equality to which his argument now moves. It arises from his saying, already quoted, that it is illusory to wish that all may have identical opportunities. It is nevertheless proper, he adds, that the highest social conditions shall not be closed to anyone, and

that in whatever *social* structure men are involved, they should have the same opportunities to achieve—each one according to his effort and condition—their human fullness, those fruits of wisdom and human virtue whose savour is not identical, but similarly good in each, whether he spends his life in working the earth, in philosophy, or in governing the State. Thus such notions as that of equality of opportunity or equality of conditions, which equalitarians would make chimerical, become true and proper if they are understood in the sense not of an equality pure and simple, but of a *proportional* equality.

This proportional equality, Maritain claims, is justice itself—the only justice that takes into account the relations between the social whole and its parts—the only justice, we are inclined to add, which is at once firm and flexible. And Maritain brings this part of his argument to its climax with a splendid similitude. Thinking of the essential unity of mankind as a root, and of inequalities as branches springing from humanity's deeply rooted tree, he says of proportional equality that

it is a new kind of equality which, by virtue of justice, friendship and human compassion and by virtue of the communication they provoke, is realized in the fruit.

The human value, the practical application, of this essay overflows the banks of its dialectic. In ages less hurried than our own, it would have irrigated and fertilized the contemporary mind, for it satisfies a great need—the need of those who are neither totalitarians nor fanatical levellers for a

philosophical presentation of their central and liberal purpose.
On either flank of this great body of opinion there have arisen
totalitarians of the Left and of the Right who are at one in
their belief that government should be by the dictatorship of a
party.   Against them stands the democratic ideal which, for
lack of philosophical restatement in positive terms, has become
perilously weakened.   The source of its weakness is that
thousands of those who subscribe or believe that they subscribe
to it have become confused in their minds on the problem
of equality.   They say that, as democrats, they " believe in
equality ", or that, as Christians, they wish " to break down
the barriers of class-privilege ", or that " in the new world
everyone must have an equal chance ", and because they have
not paused to ask what they themselves mean by equality,
and have indeed assumed that the word is self-explanatory,
they have become, in many instances, a prey to those who,
advocating a doctrine that must enslave the individual to whatever party is successful in usurping the State, play upon the
democratic confusion between proportional equality and crude
equalitarianism.   That Maritain's essay should become a text-
book of the majority is not to be expected, but books that few
have read for themselves have had before now great influence
on the world, and this essay, if statesmen and teachers would
ponder and distil and interpret it, might have such an influence.

To offer to men what Maritain means by Proportional
Equality is to set before them a purpose which, in the first
place, is not chimerical as the equalitarian purpose is, and which,
secondly, may be struggled for and attained without that
suppression of the fundamental rights of the human person
which every form of totalitarianism requires.   It assumes
and maintains those rights, and the " fruitful inequalities "
inherent in them, but it seeks continually a reconciliation of
those inequalities and requires a steady movement, not towards
identical opportunities for all men, which, since men differ in

their powers, would be an embarrassment to men of humble capacity and insufficient to men of great capacity, but towards an equal opportunity to each man to bring *his* gifts to fruit. Proportional Equality—if we seek an illustrative metaphor—may, perhaps, be best understood as the purpose, within his own sphere, of a wise and progressive educationist who knows that to drag all his pupils into a single classroom and to impose upon them all the same syllabus is to make nonsense of education and travesty of democratic principle. His aim is to bring each pupil's gifts to fruit. Therefore, recognizing a division of gifts, he divides his pupils, and gives to each division opportunity proportionate to its members' true needs, careful always that, as their gifts develop, his pupils may transfer themselves from one division to another. Maritain applies this proportionate idea to life itself, looking always towards a purpose which totalitarians and levellers repudiate and which he has the courage to describe as " an aristocracy of personal work that pays back the good effects of its labour for common use ". This purpose, the humane alternative to tyrannical obscurantism, is given its philosophical and Christian justification in this great Frenchman's essay.

CONCLUSION

No treaty of alliance between romantics and classicists has emerged from the preceding discussion, nor is any such treaty to be desired. These pages will have served their purpose if they have suggested that romantics and classicists, being men of spirit, have a common enemy in those whose conception of human nature is altogether different from theirs, and who deny that the word " spirit " has meaning.

In saying this, I, who am not a member of the Church of Rome and cannot therefore rely upon authority valid for Maritain, am bound so far to define my terms as to say that by the word " spirit ", in this context, I mean *at least* an element in each man, distinct from his mind and body, which both has expression on earth through his mind and body, and is his line of communication and apprehension, his link, with a Reality not of this world. The spirit pertaining to each man is thought of by me as being part of the Spirit of Man, or, since to speak quantitatively of spiritual things is misleading, I would rather say: " as being of the same substance with the Spirit of Man "; and this Spirit of Man, though it is not knowable by our intellects only, I think of as being not far beyond our intellectual grasp, as being accessible to our faculty of wonder, and communicable, though not fully communicable, in poetry. It is, if I may be allowed to use language so inadequate, a proximate degree in that hierarchy which extends from our sensuous perception to the Supreme Reality. It is an early rung in the ladder of apprehension.

A romantic, seeking a philosophy, a religion, a faith, which transcends and harmonizes the " felt disharmony " of our life here, and a classicist whose task, as he sees it, is to apply a

philosophy and faith already accepted to the transcendence
and harmonizing of a disharmony equally felt by him though
differently analysed, have in common that they both recognize
the existence of the ladder of apprehension and of the spiritual
element in man.   Collective materialists deny these things.
For them no ladder extends beyond the mind.   They are as
free, therefore, to operate upon the mind as they are to operate
upon the body.   If, in pursuit of an end which they consider
expedient, they enslave the body, they will as readily enslave
the mind, for, in their view, the mind is only a part of the
body, and not, as it is for romantics and classicists, an instrument and a vehicle of the spirit.

Therefore I think that civilization is confronted by a threat
to all charity and gentleness, and to the order of sanity itself.
The Spirit of Man is threatened with deliberate corruption in
its tabernacle of the mind.   The purpose of collective materialists is to deprive men of their will to exercise will, and to
anæsthetize in them that sense of individuality, of their being
each one a spiritual being, of which the effect is a transcendence
of materialism.   In days gone by, the pursuers of this purpose
and the resisters against it might have been regarded as men
engaged, with equal weapons, in a struggle between two
opposed philosophies.   But the weapons are no longer equal.
Physical science is obtaining, and appears in the Soviet trials
to have already obtained, power to deprive the mind of will
and judgement.   In face of this threat, the world is required
to fight a battle more far-reaching than any that has yet been
fought against tyrants who dreamed of nothing worse than
the torture and enslavement of the body.   In slavery, there
is a hope of escape or emancipation.   Even in torture, there
is the possibility that it will cease, that wounds will heal and
health be renewed.   But who shall minister to a mind in
which disease has been scientifically induced?   Or who create
again a dead individuality?   Those who would forbid to

romantics and classicists alike the will to transcendence are denying to mankind the possibility of self-renewal. In another and greater language, it may be justly said that their purpose is to exile man from Grace. It is a purpose as old as serpents, but never before have its devotees been equipped with earthly weapons so powerful.

V. INSTANCES

BERGSON AND THE MARITAINS or *Liberty from Materialism*

HUMANE COUNSELLORS or *The Liberty to Ask Questions*

THE SILKWORM AND THE LOOM or *The Liberty to Mind One's Own Business*

A WRITER AMONG PAINTERS or *The Liberty to Communicate*

SANCTITY AND SONG or *The Liberty to Draw Back Curtains*

BERGSON AND THE MARITAINS
OR
LIBERTY FROM MATERIALISM

" We found the philosopher in the full flush of his youthful glory." It is a glorious opening to a chapter and lifts the heart of the reader who comes upon it. At last, he says, here is a book which is concerned with neither guns nor butter nor collective materialism of any kind, but with the search for truth. In such a book there is always a danger that it may become either rhapsodic or dry—either an unbalanced eulogy of a particular philosopher or a dusty dispute between parties or schools. Madame Maritain's volume is neither of these things. It comes very near to being a fusion of the romantic with the classical spirit, and is valuable as an instance of the theme just now discussed.

The sentence which has been quoted might have been written by Héloïse, but was in fact written lately in America by a Frenchwoman, by birth a Russian Jewess, who became the wife of Jacques Maritain thirty years ago. The volume's unfortunate title *, which might serve any set of chatty reminiscences, must be allowed to deceive no one. Madame Maritain has no interest whatever in the smart, the powerful, the fashionable or the clever, and though, when she wishes to do so, she can make a scene visible by the simplicity of her descriptions, it is never with appearances that she is primarily concerned but with the reality behind or within them. It happens that, while she was studying at the Sorbonne, she fell in love with a fellow-student, Jacques Maritain, who, developing

* *We Have Been Friends Together*. Memoirs by RAÏSSA MARI-
TAIN. Translated by JULIE KERNAN. Longmans.

the tradition of Bergson, has since become one of the great
philosophers of Europe; and it would have been easy for her,
in describing their early days together, to have allowed her
narrative to lose its poise by laying too strong a romantic
emphasis on their personal relationship or by too self-con-
sciously abstaining from it.   Instead she says:—

> We had been engaged for at least two years when we decided
> to get married without waiting for the end of Jacques's studies.
> Our engagement took place in the simplest way, without any
> proposal.   We were alone in my parents' living-room.   Jacques
> was sitting on the rug, close to my chair; it suddenly seemed to
> me that we had always been near each other, and that we would
> always be so.   Without thinking, I put out my hand and stroked
> his hair; he looked at me and all was clear to us.   The feeling
> flowed through me that always—for my happiness and my salva-
> tion (I thought precisely that, although then the word " salvation "
> meant nothing to me)—that always my life would be bound up
> with Jacques's.   It was one of those tender and peaceful feelings
> which are like a gift flowing from a region higher than ourselves,
> illuminating the future and deepening the present.   From that
> moment our understanding was perfect and unchangeable.

There is a school of criticism, left over from a dead fashion,
which would disapprove of this passage.   It is neither desic-
cated nor violent.   It neither quibbles nor screams.   As
Tolstoy said of Turgenev, it is not " restive ".   For that
reason it has been quoted here as an instance of the directness
and fearlessness of the author's approach to her subject,
whether that subject is personal or philosophical.

   In one aspect, her book is an account of her own and her
husband's conversion to Rome.   That their intellectual and
spiritual journey led to their being baptized on 11 June 1906
at the Church of St. John the Evangelist in Montmartre is an
important fact in the narrative, but the narrative has an importance which, from the point of view of those of us who are
not of their Church, transcends—or perhaps we should say
" includes "—their conversion.   For whether or not a man
chooses the path chosen by them, it is impossible to read Mme.

Maritain's book without being struck by the similarity between the condition of barrenness into which she fell and the condition in which the contemporary world finds itself.   She felt herself overwhelmed by what she describes as " the anti-metaphysical prejudices of pseudo-scientific positivism ".   The world in general would not give this name to its sickness, to its weariness of unrelated knowledge and competing half-truths, because the world in general does not think in the language of a learned philosophical student of the Sorbonne, but its sickness is the sickness by which she and Jacques Maritain were visited and from which Bergson rescued them.

We have all been accustomed by our reading of nineteenth-century literature to those crises of religious doubt which our fathers experienced.   Brought up as believers, they began to doubt their belief.   Again and again we hear how, after a period of struggle, of clinging to the faith that was decaying in them or at any rate to the forms and habits which had expressed this faith, they shook off what they had come to regard as superstition.   They decided that all truth was relative, or, rather, that there was no singleness of truth which man was capable of knowing, but only an assembly of fragments which might be measured.   This process of religious doubt was the converse of that through which the young Maritains passed.   Instead of doubting an established religion, they doubted a scepticism.   Instead of falling away, as our rationalistic fathers did, from a Church, they fell away from the Sorbonne and from the established system of thinking which at that time it represented.   This system was the result of an attempt to supply a non-metaphysical alternative to the chaos which had, in many instances, resulted from the rationalists' abandonment of faith.   The Sorbonne was fully aware of the perils of unrelated knowledge, of intellectual fragmentation.   It therefore measured the fragments and laid them side by side and, where it could, fitted them together.   But because, in contemplating the fragments, it did not acknowledge the existence of a knowable Whole, it left unanswered certain questions which became a torment to the Maritains.   Here were the fragments—but fragments of what?   What did it mean to say that they were measurable if there was nothing to which their measurements might be referred?   What did it mean to say that they were related, and to examine their relationship, if they were related only to one another?

Asking these questions, which their training at the Sorbonne had at least taught them how to formulate, Jacques and Raïssa Maritain were unhappy in the same way and for the same reasons that a great part of mankind is unhappy today. But they had the advantage, which most men have not, of knowing what was wanting in them and of knowing that it was wanting *in them*.   Human injustice was abhorrent to them; poverty, destitution, *misère*, they looked in the face without sentimentality or illusion; but they did not suppose that a remedy for these things, if it were found, would be a remedy for the unhappiness of the world.   On the subject of destitution, there is a passage from Péguy which Mme. Maritain quotes and is worth re-quoting so that none may imagine her to be a cold metaphysician aloof from the worldly sufferings of man.

It should be explained that the translator has chosen to use the English word " misery " for " *misère* " in order to distinguish " misery ", which " is the lack even of the needful ", from poverty which " is the lack of everything superfluous ". This peculiarity—would not " destitution " have conveyed the meaning?—makes the passage sound a little odd, but, because it penetrates through the fact of destitution to the idea of being destitute, it retains Péguy's quality.

Misery is a grandeur, so great that the other human greatnesses in comparison appear small; when one knows well the truly destitute, the most striking thing in them, in their very humiliation, is a certain tone of haughtiness; their humility is often only haughtiness, possessed within.   In speaking of other men they always have an air of saying: " You do not know life because you do not know misery."   It is precisely this greatness, of which they are conscious, that they cannot always bear and which goes to their heads. . . . They are condemned by the force of events to play life as a tragedy, without having the tragic temperament or genius.

It is true not of the destitute only but of all men whose earthly suffering is extreme and appears to them to be not an accident of their life but their life itself.

Péguy was writing before 1914.   Since then the world has fallen beneath a curse of violence comparable, in the life of nations, with destitution in the lives of men, and even as the present war approached its end, we learned that its final stages had yielded a revolutionary development in weapons of violence and in the abasement of science to evil, and that this development was in its infancy.   Therefore, for Péguy's particular use of *misère* in its relationship to men, a more general use may now be substituted, and what Péguy says of the " miserable man " may be applied by the despairing to civilized man.   Misery, in the wider sense of decivilization by violence, may appear to him as

not a part of his life, a part of his anxieties, which he examines in its turn and without prejudice to the others.   Misery is his whole life, it is a servitude without surcease.   It is not merely the known funeral train of privations, of illnesses, uglinesses, despairs, ingratitudes and deaths; it is a living death; it is the perpetual pain of Antigone; it is the universal penetration of death into life; it is an aftertaste of death mixed with the whole of life.

This is the anguish, the destitution of the soul, into which, if we see only the fragments of life and fail even to ask: " Fragments of what? " mankind may fall.   For a moment, when she wrote a prefatory note to this book, Mme. Maritain came near to falling into this abyss.

Yet even her preface is not despair, but a looking into the abyss and then beyond it.   The young student at the Sorbonne, the older woman who writes " there is no longer any future for me in this world ", and he among us who despairs of civilization, are all looking into the same abyss—the abyss of disintegration, of the seeming disorder of reason and the fragmentation of knowledge.   It is then necessary that we ask: " Fragments of what?"   It is necessary that we be persuaded that there is an answer, that there is a truth of which all separable truths are but the related appearances.   Though what that truth is we may not know, we must become aware that it is knowable.   How the young student became aware of this, Mme. Maritain tells with rare lucidity, and in the telling she makes it plain, as few have before her, that meta-physical thought is not what a great part of the contemporary world supposes it to be—the fantastic intellectual exercise of specialists—but a way to that harmony of which happiness, pursued in vain if pursued for its own sake, is a consequence.

It is, then, upon the young student's movement away from " pseudo-scientific positivism " rather than upon her later acceptance of Catholicism that many readers may wish to dwell, though the story of her conversion, of her own and her husband's association with Léon Bloy, and even of their differences with Péguy, is told with a candour and tenderness that will recommend it to all but those to whom religion itself is meaningless.   Indeed, many of the book's most brilliant passages are concerned with or arise from the Maritains' con-version, but they have, in a sense, a special application; they have not the universality of the chapters which, before any creed had been accepted, tell the everlasting history of how a man and a woman made their escape from spiritual sterility, how they became aware that there existed a knowable truth.

One summer afternoon they were walking together in the Jardin des Plantes, reviewing the results of their study at the Sorbonne.   They felt that the specialized scientific and philosophical knowledge they had acquired was " undermined by the relativism of the scientists, by the scepticism of the philosophers ". They reasoned about reason and were not content to seek only the visible and measurable. They felt that they and their generation were the victims of a scepticism which was " active and capable of disrupting the life of the soul ". The parallel between their condition then and the condition of that part of the present world which is most unhappy is exact. Mme. Maritain describes it as " metaphysical anguish, going down to the very roots of life " and " capable of becoming a total despair and of ending in suicide ". They said to one another what the world, in its heart, is now saying continually :—

If our nature was so unhappy as to possess only a pseudo-intelligence capable of everything but the truth, if, sitting in judgement on itself, it had to debase itself to such a point, then we could neither think nor act with any dignity. In that case everything became absurd—and impossible to accept—without our even knowing what it was in us that thus refused acceptance. . . . We cannot base our lives upon prejudices, good or bad; we need to weigh their justice and value—but after what measure? Where is the measure of all things?

This as yet was to ask too much. They had first to be persuaded that there *is* a measure of all things. Guided by Péguy, and in face of the " mountain of distrust existing between the two institutions ", they crossed the street from the Sorbonne to the Collège de France. It was there that they " found the philosopher in the full flush of his youthful glory ". He had not yet published his *Creative Evolution*.

We went to Bergson's classes filled with overwhelming curiosity and a sacred expectation. We returned, carrying our little bouquet of truths or of promises, as though vitalized by healthful air—exuberant, prolonging to greater and still greater lengths our commentaries upon the master's teachings. Winter was passing away; spring was coming.

How thought shines and glows in France! From generation to generation, how her intellect is illumined by her spirit!

How she gives, and, more wonderfully, how she makes men capable of receiving from her! Mme. Maritain was not a native of France, and yet the voice is the voice of Héloïse.

It is impossible, in such an essay as this, to trace the influence of Bergsonism upon her. Whoever will study it in the light of Jacques Maritain's preface to the second edition of his *Philosophie Bergsonienne* will best appreciate it. In this preface, written after his conversion, Maritain explained how, after prolonged struggle, he had failed to harmonize

the " conceptual " pronouncements of that theological faith which had recently opened my eyes and the philosophical doctrine to which I had had such passionate devotion during my student years, and to which I owed my delivery from the idols of materialism.

It is a brave and, at the same time, a sad renouncement. The light it throws upon the past is in that grateful word " delivery ". Mme. Maritain speaks of Bergson in the same sense. Though she also is now critical of certain aspects of his teaching, she recognizes that it " supplied us with the very possibility of metaphysical work ". His pupils learned from him that man was capable of truly knowing reality, that through intuition he might attain to the absolute and " truly, absolutely, *know what is* ". The very word " absolute " is one from which men shrink if they are not philosophers by profession. Yet it is true that none can look upon his contemporaries, or into his own heart, without recognizing that the world is sterile for lack of the assurance with which Bergson impregnated his pupils: the assurance that there is a measure of all things and that man, though he may not attain to truth, is not by his nature debarred from attaining to it. To know this is the remedy for fanaticism as it is for despair, fanaticism, even at its best, being often spiritual pride in a particular truth upheld at the expense of truth itself.

HUMANE COUNSELLORS
OR
THE LIBERTY TO ASK QUESTIONS

AMONG the queer lacunæ in our system—so queer and so easily remediable that one is tempted to ask whether it has ever been noticed—is the absence of men of thought *as such* and men of imagination *as such* from the nations' councils. The italics are important. None but a disgruntled fool or a disappointed partisan would suggest that thought and imagination have not a place in those councils. Neither great industry nor the Labour movement nor the bleak Treasury itself is empty of wise men. Nevertheless it is true that those wise men, humane though they often are, have won their places and hold them for reasons other than their humanism, and are, in nearly all instances, beset by practical, administrative tasks which stand between them and the larger meditation. The consequence is that they find it harder and harder to avoid the twin errors against which, in the year 1943, Smuts issued a warning—that of over-simplifying and that of concealing under slogans and catchwords the extreme difficulties of the truth.

The Peace Conference met in January, 1919, and it dissolved in May. Within that period, by a process of side-tracking real issues and over-simplifying others, we produced the peace treaty, and I am sure if we were to follow the same procedure in the situation before us today in the world, or the situation which will be before us at the end of this war, we shall move to even greater disasters than we have seen in the past.

It was a stern warning—and not only against the hasty patching-up of peace treaties. It is a warning to every Royal Commission, every Board of Directors, every Inter-Allied and Inter-Service Conference, every group of men who sit together to determine policy, against that besetting sin of all committees—" the process of side-tracking real issues ". Much less often than the heathen suppose is this process the result of laziness or ill-will. It springs, in most instances, from failure to see, amid the conflict of experts and the clamour of partisans, what the real issue is. The trouble is not so much that the wrong answers are given as that the right questions are not asked.

Governments are not, as the querulous believe, always fools. They are aware of this difficulty. In an endeavour to overcome it where problems of deep policy are concerned, they seek advice. Royal Commissions are set up. Ministers appoint advisory councils. Boards of directors establish subcommittees with instructions to examine a particular problem and report back. Whoever looks carefully at the constitution of these bodies will note that one element is nearly always absent—a humane counsellor appointed for his quality of humanism. Royal Commissions, for example, generally include (and rightly include) experts on various aspects of the problem to be examined, representatives of the principal interests likely to be affected, and a sedate chairman. One or two " fancy " members are sometimes added—a representative, perhaps, of some worthy and slightly relevant society or one of those industrious ladies, loved by the paragraphists, who make their voyage to Parliament in a convoy of perambulators. This, no doubt, is as it should be, and yet not all that it might be. Why is no humane counsellor appointed: a philosopher, a historian, a scholar, a painter—yes, even a poet or a story-teller, the whole value of whose presence would be that he was not a statistical expert, and did not represent a Church, a party or a society, and was not the mother of six? He might ask the questions, leading to " the real issue ", which the others forgot to ask, for it is of the essence of humanism and of all art to ask questions governing the relationship of reality to appearances and of truth to half-truth. It might be helpful, and would certainly enliven many a dull minute-book, to have them asked. But, it will be said, such men are, in fact, consulted—and, indeed, they are on occasion; they are consulted on their own craft. If the question is: shall painting be taught in schools?—painters will be asked their opinion. If St. Paul's Cathedral needs grouting, architects will sit down with engineers. If ever, which heaven forbid, there were a Royal Commission on sonnets, a poet would be invited to the party. That is not the point, but rather that on subjects unrelated to their own crafts the counsel of such men would be of value, and is not asked.

That many practical men will smile a little at the very notion of inviting a poet to be a director of a great industrial company or a story-teller to membership of an advisory council on foreign policy or education is itself a criticism of our society; for the suggestion is neither fantastic nor without precedent. Extremely adroit princes did not regard as valueless the opinion of Voltaire, and the author of *Paradise Lost* was not considered a helpless dreamer. If such judgements were of value in days when the world was comparatively simple and statesmanship leisurely, of how much greater value would they be today! At Versailles, where the fate of dynasts was in question, would it not have been a refreshment to the political mind if it had been possible to look up from some deadlock of the experts and say: " Well, Mr. Hardy, what do you think? " It is very reasonable to say of political judgement what Walter Raleigh once said of poetic expression: " I like my poetry good. If I cannot get it good, I like it *rum*; and Hardy is *rum*." Hardy's political comment also would have been rum, and to meditate on the effect that it might have had on President Wilson is to indulge in one of the most stimulating of historical dreams. For Hardy's mind, subtle and yet direct, fiercely independent and yet almost inhumanly modest, was precisely the sort of mind that lifts the diplomatic gramophone out of its groove. He would not have attempted to challenge or to conciliate. Probably, he would have felt extremely uncomfortable and not have spoken except when he was spoken to, but the very fact that he was not an expert, not a diplomat, not a practiser of the political crafts, but the keeper of his own speculative wisdom, would have driven men, in his presence, to seek " the real issue ". Nothing is so powerful in the company of men of divided mind as the influence of a whole man, selfless and dedicated.

Consider the same problem on a humbler plane. A great industrial company has to decide whether it shall convert its plant so that it may produce machine-tools of Type B instead of machine-tools of Type A. Of what value to them is the opinion of a humanist? Of none. And if industry is to be thought of as depending solely upon such questions as this, upon what may be called technical and competitive questions, then the Board requires no advice except upon the technique of production and marketing. In fact, industry does not work in a vacuum, but in a political and social atmosphere. It can no more insulate itself from modern society than a nation can insulate itself from the modern world, and every mind in industry fit to be called a mind is occupying itself more and more with a complex series of external and internal relationships and is trying to discern the values by which these relationships are and ought to be governed. The same is true of the great organizations of labour. Leave aside the question of their direct parliamentary influence. Even in the strictly industrial sphere, their concern is not narrowly industrial. Like private employers, like Government itself, they touch human lives, they touch the nation. There are few decisions of theirs, or of any board of directors, which do not affect, directly or at a remove, the whole community's way of life. Yet at board meetings and at labour congresses this communal inter-dependence is often treated as if it did not exist, not because the men there are blind or ignorant or selfish but because they are too professional, too much of a kind, too closely hedged in by the conventions of their near-duty, as diplomats are by the conventions of theirs. Their difficulty is the old one which arises again and again in every ward of modern life—the difficulty of distinguishing between long-term statesmanship and short-term policy, between wisdom and astute practice.

When such difficulties appear and are not overcome, but suffered to lead on to industrial strife by which the community suffers, the little, sharp commentators of Left or Right cry " Villainy! " They say that the men on strike are traitors, or that the employers are tyrants, or that the Government is abject and cowardly. Sometimes a part of one of these accusations may be true. More often they are all lies. All that has happened is that men who have superficially an opposed interest and, underlying it, a common interest, have been, as experts and advocates, so absorbed by their attempt to combat (or to conciliate) the opposed interest that they have not looked beyond it, and so " by a process of side-tracking the real issue and over-simplifying " have produced industrial war. Both sides hate it, and yet they succumb to the same difficulty again and again. It is very odd. If they are confronted by a legal problem that is beyond them they will take opinion of the Bar; if their factories need reorganizing they will pay great fees to rationalizers; if one of their technical processes disappoints them, they will build a city of experimental laboratories in an attempt to correct it. But where the difficulty that baffles them is humane, they will not consult a humanist; where it is a problem of the imaginative interpretation of relative values, they will not turn to an artist or a philosopher. Abana and Pharpar are their technical rivers and they will navigate them with elaborate care, but nothing will induce them to wash in Jordan. Your advice, Milton? Your judgement, Voltaire? Well, Mr. Hardy, what do you think?

A lively reader of these essays who has observed how often, in one form or another, they have urged that an artist's business is with his art, may be momentarily astonished by the course the present argument has followed. Do you really contend, he may ask, that an artist should entangle himself in business and politics, that he should allow his fallow-periods to be interrupted by a summons to a board meeting or a Royal Commission? Certainly he ought not to entangle himself to the extent of pretending to be what he is not—a business man or a politician. If it were in either of these capacities that he was invited to attend he would be bound to refuse. His duty is not to advocate any political or economic cause; his concern is with the Tree of Life, not with the Tree of Knowledge; he exists to impregnate the imagination, not to instruct it; to fluidify, not to congeal it; to preserve and proclaim its holiness, not to impose upon its divine infallibility his fallible morals. But as it is true of saints that some best follow their light as enclosed contemplatives and some as members of an order that has traffic with the world, and neither is to be despised or forbidden, so it is true of artists that they may serve God and man by more means than one, by participation as well as by withdrawal, provided always that, when they participate, they preserve, as the saints have done in the market-place, their own faithful vocation, seeing only with its eyes, answering only with its voice.

If they do this, what may, at first sight, appear to others as their arrogance will prove to be their humility. Faithful to their own vocation they will respect the skills of others and

attempt neither to imitate nor to usurp them.   They will not
try to teach a diplomat diplomacy or an industrialist his trade;
they will not compete with the world on the world's own
ground or seek notoriety from its controversies; but will be
true always to their own spiritual intuitions, leaving to Cæsar
the things that are Cæsar's.   It will be their task to give their
counsel, his to apply or to reject it, as princes have always
applied or rejected the counsel of their wise men, their
prophets.   Though none may justly question an artist's right
to withdraw from what are loosely called practical affairs, none
can forbid him—nor is he called upon to forbid himself—to
give counsel that is asked of him in recognition and not in
denial of his own vocation, for in the contemporary world
artists and humanists are heirs of the prophets and it is in
deafness to them that the people perish.

It remains, then, to ask how artists are to be chosen if they
are to be restored to the nation's councils, and how they are
to be used.   The answer to both questions is: " Simply—as
you would choose and use a friend."   The basis of choice
cannot be fame; to appoint an artist to an Advisory Council
because his repute may dress the window would be to corrupt
the whole design.   Nor is anything to be gained by considering his qualifications external to his art—that he happens to
have taught school, if the subject be education, or that he
happens to be a good mathematician, if the question be of
currency.   He is not being chosen as an educationist or as an
authority on currency; his knowledge or half-knowledge of
either subject is irrelevant.   He is being brought in not
because he resembles or competes with or balances those who
will sit at the table with him but because he differs from them
and differs from them in particular ways inherent in his vocation.   He is being chosen—or else it were better not to
choose him at all—by some great Prince or Minister, by some
enlightened industrialist, because the chooser believes in his

heart that man cannot live by bread alone or policy thrive on knowledge alone, and that to supply the deficiency it is worth while to take the risk of jester or genius. Therefore the artist to be looked for is not he who is visibly the most talented or the most spectacular or the most assertive, but he that is most profoundly dedicated and in whose wisdom there shines, by reason of this dedication, that quality which for want of a better name we call childlike—by which we mean unshadowed by the prison-house or at any rate not in league with the gaolers.

Men seek the counsel of judges on subjects unconnected with law, and in England the people will trust a judge to override their own prejudices where they will trust no one else on earth. Whenever the Executive is in doubt of an issue, and public opinion is so hot and confused that no decision by experts will quiet it, a judge of the High Court is asked to conduct an inquiry, and controversy is hushed. Why? As a man, a judge is as weak, vicious or fallible as other men are, but, as judge, there is an absolutism in him, a sacred truth, to deny which would be, for him, the impossible because the unimagined sin. It is not he that is just, but that justice of which he is the dedicated instrument. An artist's value is in the same kind with his, though of a different application. There is in him also an absolutism, a sacred truth of perception. Question him as an artist and he cannot but speak it. Why, when the world is burning and the spirit of man is choking out its life in the smoke of knowledge, will no Prince, no President, send for his prophet and say: " Tell me what you see "? It would often be hard to interpret and apply the answer, but ease of application has never, since the Sermon on the Mount, been a test of truth's efficacy; and the question itself is one that it might be the world's salvation to ask.

THE SILKWORM AND THE LOOM
OR
THE LIBERTY TO MIND ONE'S OWN BUSINESS

MAY we once before the leaves of autumn fall put away perplexities? In an empty chair near at hand a breeze flaps the pages of the morning newspaper, exposing the headlines. Its columns and the heart of man are heavy with problems, the near and the far; the mind is puffed up with its puny stratagems. May it for an hour rest from them? Here is a garden which, though bricked in among city walls, is green and silent. There are branches enough to bow to the small wind and play with it, and there is sun enough now and then to throw a dapple on the page. It is such a morning as would in childhood have been endless in an endless succession of mornings. So it might be still, if the restless grappling mind would let go its hold and cease to argue. The inverted flower-pots, the watering-cans, and the sleepy cat have patient, timeless claims. We fuss too much, are over-proud of our paltry contrivances. The Chinese sage who wrote two thousand seven hundred and twenty-three years ago, and whom Miss Helen Waddell translated, went not far enough. What he said of women— for he was an anti-feminist—has a salutary application to the human race :—

> What does she in affairs of State?
> Her place is in the inner room.
> Her wisdom doth least hurt in this,
> To mind the silkworm and the loom.

Not her wisdom only. We write pamphlets. We are for ever curing the world of what we conceive to be its naughtiness. We sell the ointment of spikenard for three hundred pence that they may be given to the poor. We permit the breeze to expose to us the headlines of the morning newspaper. The sleepy cat yawns. The silkworm is neglected.

The " inner room " is to be interpreted as a man's personal life, the " silkworm and the loom " as emblems of activity appropriate to his natural talent. It is among the chief wastages of all social upheavals that they drive him out of his inner room, out of his home, into that dreadful wilderness, barren of all true life, in which every one is busy on a task not his. Worse than this, worse than the destructive necessity of it, is the idea, which springs up and grows like a weed on the rubbish heap of collective thought, that any attempt to pre-serve the inner room is wrong, that a woman ought to unsex herself in the cause of utility, and that men who cultivate their personal lives are guilty of anachronism.

How many there are who cannot be satisfied except by a maximum disturbance! They would disturb Joan of Arc at her prayers to tell her, in tones of sprightly patriotism, that there was a war on. With a corresponding phrase, they excuse all their domestic incompetence. They create also a snobbery of hardship, affecting contempt for anyone who has been less bombed, or in peacetime less harassed, than them-selves. The sight of a girl in a pretty frock or of a man in flannels or of a group of holiday-makers in a meadow exas-perates them. They are the busybodies of the earth, the Gauleiters of the parish-pump, who, bored by the emptiness of their own inner rooms, must for ever be knocking at other men's doors. Wars and revolutions are their opportunity to do harm righteously. The cat has a grand contempt for them. They would regiment him if they could, make him walk devotedly to heel, dress him up as something that he is not. The unforgivable sin, by their standard of conduct, is, in an artist, to be an artist, in a woman to be a woman, in a cat to be a cat. Men, except very old soldiers, are clay in their hands; women, by heaven's grace less conformable animals, will elude them in the end; but no one resists them so well as the cat. He carries his inner room about with him. He does not perform tricks. All his activities are " appropriate to his natural talent ".

A cat may be admired but not imitated, but it is possible that even we should advance a little way towards his perfection:—

> I sit alone,
> And clear thoughts move in me,
> Pictures, now near, now far,
> Of transient fantasy.
> Happy I am, at peace
> In my own company.

The poem of De la Mare opened by that gentle stanza, having passed through the dread of life " dark with horror and fear ", is resolved in this:—

> Only love can redeem
> This truth, that delight;
> Bring morning to blossom again
> Out of plague-ridden night;
> Restore to the lost the found,
> To the blinded, sight.

—and is it not true that the healing love he speaks of is, precisely, that emotion which is starved, that visionary touch which is made insensitive, by our perversion of ourselves from ourselves? This, it would seem, is what De la Mare has taught always—if so pure a poet may be said to " teach "—so that there was a time not long ago when it pleased the stale vanguard to praise him with faint patronage as one who did not sufficiently address himself to the problems of their age. And now what they once thought of as " escapism " in the work of De la Mare has become the fountain of its endurance and freshness. He emerges not only as a poet of the first rank but as one who is, remarkably, a poet of his age. He is nostalgic—but it has been among the stupidities of criticism not to distinguish between nostalgias. A nostalgia for what

may, perhaps, be called the amenities of the past can be a
reason for believing that an artist, keyed to a particular set of
material conditions, has outlived it; but there is another
nostalgia—of divided man for the unity of his self, of de-
naturalized man for re-entry into his nature, of the lost for the
found, of the blinded for sight—which, above all else, exempts
a poet from the strictures of fashion, and which, at this
moment in the world's history, is the ache and agony of mankind. This is the nostalgia by which the poetry of De la
Mare is haunted:—

> What needest thou?—a few brief hours of rest
> Wherein to seek thyself in thine own breast . . .
> O foolish one to roam
> So far in thine own mind away from home!

And is not this the cry of contemporary man, driven out
from his inner room?

> Betrayed and fugitive, I still must roam
> A world where sin, and beauty, whisper of Home.

Say what you will of those two lines. Say that they are
neither political nor class-conscious and are therefore to be
condemned. But do not say that they are " uncontemporary "!
That they are not is among the principal hopes of civilization. The planners continue to plan and, in so far as their
planning is technical and administrative, they are sometimes
justified; but the planners who are constituting themselves
as intellectual drill-sergeants for the better disciplining of
mankind will find before long that, when they give their
orders, the squad will dissolve. They have mistaken the
temper of the English and of the period in which they live.
The approaching age will not be eagerly and collectively
experimental in outward, material things, for the good reason
that men are weary of the bait. In peace, as in war, they will
accept the discipline necessary for the safeguarding of their
private lives from chaos and disruption. Thrust upon them

more regimentation than that, and they will learn to tear up the forms.   They need time in which to make peace with themselves, to find their way home, to be in their inner room. Do not, O earnest Committeemen and Officials, come knocking at the door!   You may drive civilization mad.   It may spring out upon you.   Leave it in peace.   It is not reactionary or revolutionary, but it does not need your telling.   Do not bother it.   When it is ready, it will know what to do.

Meanwhile, here is a garden which, though bricked in among city walls, is green and silent.   Here, in this little patch, if we would but take it, is the way to that sanity which might make translucent all our perplexities.   If it be presupposed that there is no happiness but a new happiness, and one to be bought with a new currency, then indeed this garden is a waste of time.   Out we must go into the dusty street and stand in a queue for a patent remedy, and next, with sandwich-boards across our shoulders, parade the gutter to advertise this great good to mankind.   The alternative is to reflect that there are ages in which to be oneself is by no means to be selfish, and in which to be disinterested is the greatest service that a man may do his fellow-men.   The icy commentators have not always been kind to Alfred de Vigny's " Journal ", but his entry on 31 December 1831 should win their hearts :—

L'année est écoulée.   Je rends grâces au ciel qui a fait qu'elle se soit passée comme les autres, sans que rien ait altéré l'indépendance de mon caractère et le sauvage bonheur de ma vie.

So a good cat might have written in his wisdom.   Alfred de Vigny applies it to himself :—

Je n'ai fait de mal à personne.   Je n'ai pas écrit une ligne contre ma conscience ni contre aucun être vivant; cette année a été inoffensive comme les autres années de ma vie.

It is not spectacular, but as a comment upon his own life by one who had been born in the last months of the eighteenth century, whose boyhood had been the Napoleonic Wars, who had served in the army and was now in his thirty-second year, it has an extraordinary aptness to our present case. How many millions there are who would give all they have to be able to write on New Year's Eve what Vigny wrote then! He was accused, in attempted disparagement, of inhabiting a " *tour d'ivoire* "—a phrase that has passed down the intervening century from busybody to Gauleiter, from parrot to parrot. What is it but another name for a man's own home, for the inner room of his being, and what crime does he commit there but that of being disinterested? To be disinterested is not to be indifferent or cold or heartless or aloof. It is, rather, so to cultivate the silkworm and attend the loom that one's energies are poured into them and turned away from interference with one's fellow-men, and this, if any, is the way of sanity in a disordered and disintegrating world.

The delight of it is that it should have been prescribed not only by Miss Waddell's Chinese sage, but, in our own epoch, by Vigny of all men, for if, as assuredly he does, Vigny strikes a note in the discords of today, it is a sign and portent. He has been roughly grouped with the French Romantics, but his special gravity and tolerance—if you like, his pessimism— were classical. Notwithstanding " *le sauvage bonheur de sa vie* ", he cared for proportion as an active, necessary and fruitful virtue upon which all other virtues were dependent. Not to be " offensive ", not to write—or act—against anyone living, not to yield the independence of one's character, to be proportionate—is it to that we are coming? To those who are still reaching for a wand that shall strike out of chaos a new heaven and a new earth it may seem a negative creed, and so it might be but for the saving truth that no one yet has lived patiently in his inner room without finding treasures there. The process is hard in its austere simplicities, particularly for a generation of men who have been so long accustomed to believe that they could by their ingenuities twist fate to their purpose. They have failed. The world has crashed about them. What a temptation to talk of a new world that their ingenuities will construct! Give us, they say, one more chance! Here is our blue-print for Utopia! But by now the world is tired of them and will at all costs have relief from their perplexities.

The process is humble and simple, like all the solutions of all the problems of this world. It consists, first, in the acknowledgment of losses and the renunciation of impossible hopes —then in discovering again, and accepting as enough, those happinesses which are independent of policy. Upon them, at long last, policy may build again, and must, for man is a political animal; but his policy depends for its health upon the health and proportion of his individualism. He is not only or chiefly a political animal. He is a creature of the spirit, tormented and delighted by memories of exile from his home, and farther from home than ever he has been, but— unless all faith is delusion—now returning. There are many who see in the present years only a deepening of the exile. They feel that man is utterly committed to the prides of his collective power over nature and must now go on, calling by the name of progress his ruinous flight from himself.

There are others who still believe that this flight is the way of his salvation and may somehow—by a better regulated robotry—be turned to his advantage. But, in a garden on a summer's morning, this seems to be untrue, and witnesses so far divided as Vigny and De la Mare and the Chinese sage combine to declare its untruth. Who, of whatever creed or party, will look in his heart and deny that there has arisen, among the young and the old, a new disinterestedness, a detachment which is utterly different from scepticism or boredom or despair? Nor is it disillusionment—that was the mood of the twenties. Nor is it a casual bitterness—that was of the

thirties.   It has not yet gone far in political effect; the dis-
franchisement of intelligence and responsibility by universal
suffrage may yet, for a little while, ride it down; but there is
a new modesty in it, a willingness of men and women to cease
thinking of themselves as omnipotent masses and to apprentice
themselves one by one in callings appropriate to their natural
talent.   There is, in the air, a sense of stoical return and
rediscovery.

> All which thy child's mistake
> Fancies as lost, I have stored for thee at home—

There is a strange chance in books this morning!   Open
De la Mare, open Francis Thompson, the words " lost " and
" home " arise continually.   Is it not possible that, against
all the cries of " Reaction!   Reaction! " from those who have
led her out, the Spirit of Man is returning to her origins?   To
what end?   To whose advantage?   " Let her alone.   Why
trouble ye her? "

> Leave this vain questioning.   Is not sweet the rose?
> Sings not the wild bird ere to rest he goes?
> Hath not in miracle brave June returned?
> Burns not her beauty as of old it burned?
> O foolish one to roam
> So far in thine own mind away from home!

A WRITER AMONG PAINTERS
OR
THE LIBERTY TO COMMUNICATE

THERE is no happier relief from the pressure of over-special-
ization than to be made free of another man's workshop; but
it is necessary to be qualified for this freedom as for all others;
one must have knowledge and intuitive sympathy enough to
be able to enter into the new workshop, and see it, and feel it,
from the inside. Sometimes, and nowadays often, this is
impossible. The shop of a nuclear physicist is closed against
most of us by our inability to talk his mathematical language,
and it is among the tragedies of contemporary life that, in
many areas of learning, the great specialists are becoming less
and less able to communicate across the boundaries of their
specializations.

The development of humanism has depended always upon
men's power to move freely among the compartments of
knowledge. By this means, specializations have been related to one another. Ceasing to be prison-cells, theological,
philosophical or scientific, they have tended to become what
Leonardo and Bacon and Aquinas tried to make them: communicating rooms in a house of universal wisdom. Today,
more and more rooms in the house are barred and sealed.
Logical positivists may feel that, as philosophers, they are
disabled because they are not physicists. The conclusions of
Einstein may, with extreme difficulty, be grasped, at least in
outline, by laymen, but they must be taken on trust, for his
proofs are incommunicable except to a few familiars of his
own specialization.

It is no reassurance to say that the thought of the mystic

poets has always been incommunicable except to a few, for the poets are at least using, within its limitations, a common language. If communication breaks down between them and ourselves it is because the power of language is limited and because, in any case, they have used, and we have received it, imperfectly. In this sense, the breakdown between them and us is accidental and remediable; it is not a breakdown in the nature of things. But Einstein is using, and is compelled to use, a cipher which is inaccessible, and must remain inaccessible, except to a few; a cipher which, I venture to think, may, at certain levels, be completely inaccessible to all but himself. If this is true, or even partly true; if it is also true, in the same sense though in a different degree, that the expression of all knowledge is moving towards a condition of cipher, it would appear that Babel has come again, and perhaps for the old reasons of impiety.

But these are high matters. Those of us who are not physicists are off our ground and had better return to it.

Whoever has a special skill, whether it be that of a carpenter or a landscapist, of a farmer or a writer, knows that to have admission to another man's craft is to be refreshed in his own. One whose trade is words turns gladly to arts that are wordless, to music or painting, perhaps. They are rain in those periods of dryness, which all artists know, when thought can harden prematurely into sentences, and even experience, before it can be deployed for imaginative attack, becomes locked in some narrow defile of syntax and cadence, to wither there.

At such times, to escape from words and to penetrate a little way into the mystery of another craft is self-loss and self-renewal. It was once my fortune to live a few weeks among the vinegrowers of the Charente, and to learn something of their art and the patient craftsmanship of their barrel-makers. At another time, in Lucca, I was made free of a clockmaker's backroom, where, with an artist's equal care for his several employments, he mended clocks or made enchanted toys or, when he could, humbly pursued the art of Cellini with what precious metals he had.   But these were rare experiences, not easily to be repeated, nor had I more than a spectator's part in them.   The arrow struck deeper when it became my custom, week after week for several years, to go to a painter's studio, and draw, from his private sitters and his models, drawings which would never be exhibited, which had nothing to offer me but their sole selves, and which, therefore, commanded in me an absolute and unanxious devotion.   If one day the drawing was bad, it was bad in itself, not in the condemnation of others; if less bad, not by the encouragement of their praises.   The painter himself had the charity neither to praise nor blame nor teach me.   I owe him a great debt, for he gave me liberty from my own specialization.   I went back to my inkpot, eager and renewed.

A writer, who does not draw, may still have, in the visual arts, renewal in the same kind, provided always that he lose himself in them.   When he is invited by painters to see their work, he goes in a dual capacity—as a member of the public and as one who, in a different medium, is himself an exhibitor before the public.   Each half of him keeps the other half in order.   As a fellow-artist he learns how much painters have to endure and how little right he has to complain.   He is able to preserve at least a fond illusion that his book is read quietly by the reader's fireside—read for its own sake, and not skimmed as one of a thousand books all simultaneously demanding the reader's attention.   He imagines, too, that the reader's body is at ease, that he has a tolerable chair, that his consideration is not continually interrupted by the comments of others. And he sees, in contrast, how, at any exhibition of paint on canvas, the world picks and pecks, how one picture is condemned for being inferior to another to which it is unrelated either in purpose or in method, and how casually the world passes on. So, perhaps, if he but knew it, the world condemns his own book or closes it with a casual snap, but he is at least preserved from knowing it. Painters are witnesses of these things.

As a member of the public, instructed by his other-self that practises a different art, he learns to walk warily. In any picture he strives to distinguish the painter's intention and to understand his method; to see the work, if one may put it so, from the point of view of the brush and, still deeper, from that of the originating mind; for, though it is true that a work of art must stand or fall by its effect, it cannot make a just effect unless the spectator is *open* to it, and certainly he is closed, or half-closed, against it until he has grasped what the artist was driving at.

Apart from the pursuit of mere fashion or prestige, the error into which we most easily fall in judging a picture is precisely this—of not sufficiently caring to discover and to feel what the painter was driving at. Instead, to whichever " school " we belong, we are inclined to demand that a picture be painted within certain degrees of representation, and to condemn it because it is too representational or not representational enough, saying that it is " old-fashioned " or " new-fangled ", as if there were in this matter of representation an absolute right and wrong, as if through the whole history of painting there were not a fluctuation of " likeness " and " non-likeness ". Another trap lying in wait for judgement is that of praising or condemning, not the picture itself, but its subject. Each of us, being human, is more easily won by some subjects than by others; each of us, having inherited a convention or rebelled against it, is most at ease at some particular point on the representational scale between extreme " likeness " (whatever we may take that to mean) and pure design of form and colour; but though these preferences are the best of reasons for deciding whether or not to buy a picture and live with it, they ought not to lead us to say out of hand that a picture is good or bad. Its goodness or badness depends upon the value and nature of the artist's vision and upon his skill in expressing it. Of these two factors we must form our own difficult estimate; and assuredly we cannot do so unless we have first striven to see the work of art with sympathy—that is to say, not against the artist but with him, from the point of view of his mind and brush, caring more to yield to his degree of representation than to stick fast in our own, and caring greatly to discover *his* interest in his subject. Even the dullest mayor and corporation can be exciting for a man with eyes, and we must be within the artist's eyes before we dare to say that his picture is meaningless.

This is how a writer would have his work appreciated, and in a picture-gallery, as he stands before a canvas, he does not allow the " member of the public " in himself to be hasty or casual or to speak the little empty words of praising or cursing that are too easily spoken. Instead, he either suspends judgement and passes on, or calls upon all the intuition and knowledge he has. There are pictures to which he can discover no response in himself. They seem to have no genuine impulse within them, to be but tired picture-making or, at the opposite extreme, to seek only to astonish groundlings. He is tempted to use of them the two words that are, of all, the most perilous in criticism: " dishonest ", " insincere "—words that are seldom justified, for the great labour of art is not lightly undertaken. It is better to say: " I do not understand this man yet ", and to pass on without condemning him; or, alternatively: " This man seems to me too smooth, half-dead, faultily faultless," and to remember Andrea. To remember, above all, that no art is bad because it is not " contemporary " or good because it is. A belief that to be " contemporary " is in itself a virtue arises from the fact that certain artists who do not use a contemporary idiom are plainly imitative of

past masters; it seems not to occur to men who fear to be out
of fashion that many who employ a contemporary medium
are as plainly imitative of present masters, or that those who
adhere to an earlier tradition may not be imitative at all, but
more deeply original in that they are trying to grow a new
branch from the original trunk rather than a new twig from
the latest or " contemporary " branch.   As an indication of
æsthetic value, " contemporary " and " uncontemporary " are
uncritical and prejudicial words.   The use of them leads, on
both sides of controversy, to hardness of heart, and to harden
one's heart against a genuine artist is one of those sins which
strike at the whole good of the world.

Even in the flurry and jostle of a fashionable exhibition of
pictures, a writer feels this continuously and is on his guard.
His imagination carries him from the crowded wall to the
solitary studio, from the charged to the empty canvas, from
the canvas to the hand, from the hand to the mind; and
slowly, through fellow-feeling and his own experience of the
empty sheet of paper and of the sentences which with such
passion and stress and hope and grief are written upon it, he
begins to feel the joy, the attainment, the falling-short of the
picture before him and to know a little of what it was to have
painted it, from the taking up to the laying down of the brush.
Even so, his inescapable prejudices or his too small knowledge
of the painter's craft may distort his view of this particular
canvas, but at least he will have saved himself from the sin of
hardness of heart.   He may have failed to understand, but he
will have laid himself open to understanding, and no artist,
in whatever medium, can demand of the public more than this.
He may hope for more, he may expect more, but he cannot
demand more.   He and Time must do the rest.

That writers have often an intuitive sympathy with the arts
of painting and draughtsmanship is presumably among the

reasons for there being a long tradition of pleasant and productive friendship between men who write and men who paint. The strength of that tradition is as evident today as it was in the early years of the New English or, in Paris, at the café tables of the Nouvelle Athènes, and it may be traced back much farther, through Reynolds's dinner-parties, to the Kit-cat Club and beyond. What writers have to contribute to the association is, on the surface, fairly clear—a desire to understand and to interpret painting as well as it may be interpreted in words; but evidently the painters' contribution to it is not, and cannot be, in the same kind. It is possible for a writer, if not to describe a picture, yet, as MacColl so often proved, to enable others to see it for themselves, to awaken or deepen appreciation of it; but it is not possible for a painter to perform a like service for a book. He can illustrate, but he cannot, in the highest expository sense, criticise it in paint, and it is doubtful whether, in most cases, even were it possible, he would care to do so. Painters are seldom interested in the technical process of writing as writers so often are in the technical process of painting. Moore would discourse for hours, and with passionate interest, on the technical aspect of Steer's work, but if Steer had been told that Moore, in his old age, once walked four miles to discuss with a friend how a double relative should be removed from a sentence, he might have asked: " What is a double relative ? " but would more probably have gone to sleep.

That there is a patient craftsmanship of writing is often forgotten by all but professional writers and sometimes even by them. It is not surprising. Up to a point, anyone can write. You dip your pen and, as the heathen will have it, you " say what you have to say ". The difficulties of painting are more obvious. Even the most daring submit to an apprenticeship; there are schools and masters; it is, indeed, generally recognized, even by the heathen who are blind to the architecture of prose, that there is something to be learned in the matter of laying on paint. And a little of what there is to be learned may be taught, may be visually demonstrated, while almost nothing of what is to be learned about writing may be taught in schools. The writer's craft is desperately elusive; even its elements are less seizable than the painter's. Few pause to discuss, because in truth none can say with precision, what uses of syntax lie at the source of Addison's lucidity, whereas it is possible to say with much greater concreteness how Constable produced a particular effect of light. Whatever it is that painters bring to the relationship between writers and themselves, it is certainly not a special eagerness to penetrate and reinterpret the art of writing.

And yet it remains probably true that painters contribute more than they receive. A writer has extraordinary stimulus from their companionship. In the first place, how enviable they are! They can stand back from their work at any stage in the process of composition and see it whole—a thing that no writer can ever do. His work slides away from him page by page as he turns it, sentence by sentence as he writes it; his uncompleted form must be carried always in his memory; but theirs is ever before them, and what they do in this instant, each actual movement of their brush, is at once seen in its relationship with what they laid upon the same canvas an hour or a month ago. This power of theirs to eliminate the element of time from the construction of their work gives them a freedom which, in their company, is communicated to a writer. Their art delights and refreshes him by its solving of problems related to, and yet wonderfully different from, his own—so nearly related in essence and yet so different in practice that to consider them is often to see in a new and revealing light some difficulty that has hitherto baffled him. He may observe, for example, how often, when a painter is dissatisfied with the passage under his hand and weariness or discouragement settles upon him, he seeks the same remedy. He puts down his brush, comes clear of his easel, withdraws his eye and his mind from the canvas and the problems which have accumulated upon it, and, sitting down quietly, contemplates the model or the landscape. What in fact he has done is to cease altogether to think in terms of treatment and return deliberately to the apprehension of nature. While his brush was in his hand, the model and his painting were, through his mind, in a continuous relationship. Gradually the emphasis of that relationship had fallen more and more upon his painting; the technical problems involved in it had engrossed him; the model had become not the spring of his act of painting but an increasingly remote axis of reference; in brief, he had begun to paint intellectually, out of his head, not out of his visual sense.

Now, withdrawn from his canvas, looking at the model only and his re-imagining of the thing seen, he has fallen back upon his visual sense, has returned to his origins, and is asking, not the removed questions of treatment, but those original questions which, appearing urgently to him, first made him a painter. A writer, aware of this, becomes aware also that, as a painter may be entangled and alienated by a problem of paint, so may he himself be alienated from the natural origins of his art by a problem of words, and he says: " It is high time that I too should ' return to the senses '—not to the visual sense only but to all five "; and, at his desk that night, taking up again the paragraph that has for so long fascinated and baffled him, he finds that what is wrong with it is not, as he had stubbornly supposed, a fault of verbal structure but the plain fact of its having used the names but not the smell of flowers, the words spoken by a woman but not her voice's sound, the gesture of her hand but not its touch. So, like the painter, he stands away from his work, and sees his subject apart from any attempt to describe it.

The parallel is not exact. No art can be spoken of with

precision in terms of another, and it is, perhaps, the inexactness of the parallel between the painter's art and his own which makes it valuable to a writer. It enables him again and again to see his own problems through a simplifying glass, to come out from the intricacies of his own medium into what is—or appears to him to be—the greater directness of a painter's. Every art has in it an element of naïveté which is necessary to its health. In the struggle of practice, an artist is always in peril of losing touch with it. But though for a little while he lose it himself, he will still unfailingly recognize it as a virtue, and smile at and learn from it, in arts that he does not practise; so the recollection of what he has lost may return to him and he find it again. In no instance is this truer than in that of a writer who leaves his library for a studio. Feeling that he has grown old in words, he sees in the art of paint a spontaneity and freshness which delight and encourage him, above all a reliance on nature comparable with the reliances of children and saints. " Why does a virtuous man take delight in landscapes ? " asks Kuo Hsi in his Essay :—

It is for these reasons: that in a rustic retreat he may nourish his nature; that he may constantly meet in the country fishermen, woodcutters, and hermits, and see the soaring of cranes and hear the crying of monkeys. The din of the dusty world and the locked-inness of human habitations are what human nature habitually abhors . . .

and there are periods in the life of every writer when his heart fails him and his own medium of words presents itself to him as the din of a dusty world. From this sense of " locked-inness " the work and company of painters is an almost miraculous release. Among them, he is like a traveller in a country that is pleasant to him for three reasons: that he loves it, that at least in part he understands it, and that it is not his. Though he may envy, he cannot be jealous of its inhabitants, nor they of him. With their politics, he has no concern. If they suffer a revolution, he is not subverted. Eagerly observant though he may be of their differing individualities, he is yet aware that they have the character of their profession in the sense in which Frenchmen may be said to have the character of their nationality; and this character is one that tests and tempers and re-vitalizes his own. The essences of men are solitary, not social. What a man is, he is alone. The liberty to communicate, and to enter into other men's workshops, enables him to accept with fortitude the isolation of being man. It marks the distinction between a productive solitude and a sterile prison.

SANCTITY AND SONG
OR
THE LIBERTY TO DRAW BACK CURTAINS

" WE sat up half the night discussing it," a friend has written
to me at the end of his letter. " Saints and poets. Not saints
versus poets, but saints *and*. I can't even put my side of the
question. I think I mean how far did Traherne and Vaughan
and Herbert and the rest *know* the thing as poet, and how far
as saint. I remembered a hint of the subject in the dialogue
of your own play which I heard in London about the time of
Munich. I couldn't remember it to quote, but have looked
it up since. It's a girl talking about the people who despise
her for being a pure mathematician—and she implies that
for *pure* ' mathematician ' you can read ' poet ' or ' saint '.
What she says is : ' They think I'm not doing my job in the
world. They want me to use my brains in their way—con-
verting someone, compelling someone—politics, economics,
anti-war. . . . If you won't march in one of their regiments you
are always accused of escaping from life. Mathematics isn't
that to me. It's one of the ways of listening. . . . They don't
want to listen. They want to shout and compel. But the
world is growing tired of the regiments. They fail everywhere. The misery they want to cure by force is the misery
they have created by force—and will create again. Suddenly
men and women will grow tired of marching in step and
shouting choruses. We shall listen again when we are still.
The world is beginning to listen again. It is beginning to
watch again. In poetry, the thing comes through words.
Music says it direct. Saints and lovers know it.' That is

what the girl said in the play.* It was the last bit that had stuck in my mind. But—and here's the problem—when this "knowing" of saints is linked with the "words" of poets, is there a loss, a kind of dilution, either of the poetry or of the saintliness? Is a man like, say, George Herbert, the less saint because the more poet—and the other way round? Does the vision in each case become less pure? Is that a hopeless tangle? Or a false dilemma? It's not easy to say."

The meaning is clear enough. Everyone may ask that question in a different way and in the context of his own life, but everyone who is not blankly materialistic, who does not assert that outside sensuous experience there is nothing for saint or poet to "know" or communicate, asks it in the end. It was continually present in the mind of Francis Thompson, who gave a name to it: "Sanctity and Song". Under that title, in a brief essay, he spoke of the three Canticles—one of them "The Canticle of the Sun"—assigned to St. Francis. "To the majority of men", he said, "Saintship is an uncomprehended word. . . ."

Saintship is the touch of God. To most, even good people, God is a belief. To the saints He is an embrace. They have felt the wind of His locks, His Heart has beaten against their side. They do not believe in Him, for they know Him.

And having said that "to the many these Canticles must seem strained and fantastic things, touching in them no corresponding realities of their own experience", Francis Thompson added:—

If it is hard for such men to seize the aloofness of the purely lyrical poet, how much harder for them to seize the aloofness of the lyrical saint!

How strange a saying! Can he, Christian and poet, have believed that an intuition of holiness and poetry is the reserve

* *The Flashing Stream.* London: Macmillan, 1938. Act I. Scene 2.

of a few? If there is not, in the hearts of " the many ", a reality of their own experience, corresponding, at however great a remove, with the saintly, what earth of the human imagination has for so long, in pagan and Christian times, nurtured the mysteries? If, ultimately, the many have no ears to hear, to what audience were the parables addressed? But there leave it. It is not Francis Thompson's exclusiveness that concerns us, but rather that in spite of it he laid his emphasis on the essential link between sanctity and song—an emphasis to be found again at the opening of his essay on Shelley. There the form of it is a regret that the Catholic Church, " once the mother of poets no less than of saints . . . has relinquished to aliens the chief glories of poetry. The palm and the laurel," he says, " Dominic and Dante, sanctity and song, grew together in her soil; she has retained the palm, but forgone the laurel." He warns the Church of the peril of this division. " Beware how you misprise this potent ally, for hers is the art of Giotto and Dante; beware how you misprise this insidious foe, for hers is the art of modern France and of Byron. . . ." It must seem to many a wilful approach to an essay on Shelley. It leads Francis Thompson to speak of " Adonais " as " Shelley's inexpressibly sad exposition of Pantheistic immortality "; to quote—

He is a portion of the loveliness
Which once he made more lovely . . .

—and to ask: " What utter desolation can it be that discerns comfort in this hope, whose wan countenance is as the countenance of a despair? " Despair!—in this poem where so many of the faithful and the doubting have found their consolation! And yet his essay, however narrow we may consider its critical view of Shelley to be, remains, as literature, memorable, not only for the magnificent texture of its language, but because it is a passionate statement, in the context of Thompson's own life, of the abiding relationship—more

variable in its nature than he would allow—between the saintly
and the poetical visions.

Of this relationship, in the context of *his* own life, Shelley
was cryingly aware.   While yet a boy he " sought for ghosts "
and " saw them not " until—

> Sudden, thy shadow fell on me;
> I shrieked, and clasped my hands in ecstasy!

Compare this, for essential similarity despite the difference of
idiom, with Francis Thompson's quotation from one of the
Canticles, in which it is told how Christ struck the narrator
with a lance until he fell with pierced heart, dying on the
ground :

> But lo! I did not die;
> For my beloved Lord,
> To crown His victory,
> My life anew restored,
> So keen and fresh that I
> That moment could have soared
> To join the saints on high.

Francis Thompson asks " how many will see in this anything
but the bizarre and tortured fancy of an ascetic "—and yet the
whole value of it consists in its being not particular but universal, a penetration of the mists by which all men feel themselves to be encompassed.   It was the special genius of Shelley
to know that, in his own vision, however rare its intensity,
there was nothing alien to the nature of lesser men; he was
exalted, but not aloof, not separated.   He knew, what Francis
Thompson seems not to have guessed, that the Absolute—the
touch of God in Thompson's phrase, or Shelley's " unseen
Power "—" visits with inconstant glance each human heart
and countenance ", and it is this knowledge, this glorious
absence of spiritual exclusiveness in Shelley, which gives him
his unique quality.   His attainment is the aspiration of mankind made articulate.   The impulse of his soaring ascent is

the same which raises earthbound humanity's outreaching hand. In him, when at his celestial height, sanctity and song come near to perfect fusion, as though a skylark were made one with the light.

The word "sanctity" is now being used in a sense a little different from that in which it is ordinarily accepted. The possibility of confusion must at all costs be avoided. Men discuss the Absolute in differing languages—each using the symbols of his own creed or philosophy. Shelley, for example, speaks of "the Spirit of Beauty", Plato's Diotima in the *Symposium* of "beauty absolute, separate, simple, everlasting", and the Christian mystics of God. As there happen to be other ideas than that of Absolutism associated with all these words, confusion arises. There happen also to be other ideas than that of approach to the Absolute associated with the word sanctity. Hence it is necessary to say that the word is being used here to mean that condition of the human spirit which approaches, participates in, or in supreme instances seeks identification with, the Absolute, the reality within appearances, the essence of things.

To enter into the Absolute is among the purposes of contemplation; the contemplative strives towards it. It is also the central subject of mystical poetry; the poet strives to express it. Therefore, he yearns towards the same experience that is desired by the contemplative, but for a different reason. A contemplative desires to enter into the Absolute in order that he may dwell in it, know it, have his being in it; a poet, in order that he may communicate it. This is the similarity and this the difference between sanctity and song. And here a new subtlety appears, namely that the quality of contemplation and the quality of poetry may appear in the same man, sometimes in a man such as Shelley whom we think of primarily as a poet but who was also, in the sense in which the word is being used, a saint, a dweller in the Absolute; and sometimes in such a being as St. Teresa, who, though she was poet also, is thought of primarily as a saint.

The question asked by the letter-writer—" Is a man the less saint because the more poet and the less poet because the more saint ? "—thus analyses itself. A poet's poetry cannot become the less pure because he himself has the more deeply penetrated to its source; in brief, sanctity cannot derogate from song. But can song derogate from sanctity? The only possible answer is that, as it is not essential to sanctity, it can, but that whether it does so or not depends upon the song's nature and purpose. Contemplation has no cause of action in this world; communication with men is extraneous to it, and whatever is extraneous to it is a derogation from it. In other words, a contemplative who composes poetry *as a means of communicating with men* is by so much the less a pure contemplative, but if his poetry is for him a part of the contemplative act, and one of the means or disciplines necessary to his contemplative purpose, and so is wholly contained within that purpose, and is veritably a part of his being and not of his acting, then he is not the less saint because within his sanctity there has been song.

This, if it is true, throws light upon the nature of poetry and upon what is sometimes questioned—its " usefulness " in the world. The contemplative saint and the mystical poet may be thought of as facing in opposite ways on the same ladder—the one ascending towards the Absolute with the purpose of dwelling in it, the other descending with the object of communicating the vision of it that he has seen. But as he descends the vision fades. " Could this influence ", said Shelley, " be durable in its original purity and force, it is impossible to predict the greatness of the results; but when composition begins, inspiration is already on the decline, and the most glorious poetry that has ever been communicated to

the world is probably a feeble shadow of the original conceptions of the poet." The poet's " original conceptions " come
to him when, with the contemplative saint, he is looking upward—towards the Absolute vision; his beginning to compose
is his reversal, his turning back to earth in order to communicate with it.

There are some who speak of the enclosed and contemplative saints as " useless ", though they recognize the utility
of that saintliness which ministers to the world. Denying
the contemplative saints, they yet pay lip-service to poetry,
and do not know that they are contradicting themselves.
There are others who recognize the good of saintliness and
yet regard poetry and all art not strictly devotional as worldly
or unspiritual. The despisers of poetry quote the *Republic*
in their support, and there are many passages which appear
to justify them, but in truth what Plato attacked was not poetry,
and certainly not mystical poetry, but the poets of his own
day who, he felt, were degenerate, " for ", as Jowett says
in interpreting Plato's view, " there might be a poetry which
would be the hymn of the divine perfection, the harmony of
goodness and truth among men," and this, Plato felt, was
wanting. It therefore remains open to us, consistently with
Plato in the *Symposium* and with Shelley in his *Defence of
Poetry*, to recognize that the contemplative and the poetic
acts, though distinct and facing the one towards earth and the
other towards heaven, are complementary, as discovery and
newsbringing are complementary, and, if once this is recognized, the letter-writer's dilemma is resolved, his discord
becomes a harmony. Art is seen to be " useless " only if we
are prepared to say that contemplation is " useless ", and we
cannot say this unless we deny altogether that what the contemplative seeks is real. We may differ, as creeds and philosophies differ, about the symbols in which that reality should
be spoken of or about the nature of that reality itself; so men

may differ concerning the design and strength of an arch;
but to deny that there is such a reality to be sought for is to
reject the keystone of all arches. It is against reason to value
poetry and despise contemplation, and contrary to the loving-
kindness of the religious mind to insist upon a doctrinal rule
in art. " The cultivation of poetry ", said Shelley, " is never
more to be desired than at periods when, from an excess of
the selfish and calculating principle, the accumulation of the
materials of the external life exceed the quantity of the power
of assimilating them to the internal laws of human nature."
In such a period, more certainly even than Shelley himself,
we now live.

The divorce of art from religion has gone farther than it
had when Francis Thompson wrote—has gone farther in the
hearts of men in spite of there being, perhaps, more specifically
religious art in our time than in his. This is not a paradox.
The divorce has gone farther because while recognizing and
honouring specifically religious art—a new cathedral, for
example, or a devotional poem or play—we have moved away
from understanding in what sense it is true that art not
expressive of a creed, not employing the symbols of any
Church, and with a seemingly non-religious subject, may yet
be religious. Was not Francis Thompson too sweeping when
he spoke of " the art of modern France and of Byron " as an
" insidious foe "? " Poetry ", said Shelley again, " is indeed
something divine. It is at once the centre and circumference
of knowledge "—that is to say (if I may return to the metaphor
already used) the poet, in the time of conceiving, looks, with the
contemplative, inward to the centre, and, in the time of composition, outward to the circumference. And Shelley adds:
" Poetry is not like reasoning, a power to be exerted according
to the determination of the will." If we take his view, it
follows that art which acknowledges itself to be the communication of a central reality, an enablement of spiritual light

to shine through appearances, is, in essence, religious, whatever its apparent subject.   So terrible is the darkness of the house in which we now live, where in room after room vision has contracted and men stumble blindly amid the " materials of external life ", that we do ill to forbid any hand that draws a curtain back and admits the light, even though it be the hand of a " modern " Frenchman.   Never have sanctity, the perceiver, and song, the newsbringer, been in greater need to recognize that they are blessed of the same master, whose hand is upon either head.

Date Due
